The Power of Love^2

EXPLORING THE UNIVERSAL ENERGY
THAT WILL CHANGE YOUR LIFE

MARTIN NEIL
CAMPBELL

The Power of Love^2

ISBN Paperback: 978-0-9919873-4-4

ISBN Hardcover: 978-0-9919873-6-8

Cover Design: Thomas Threndyle, RGD

Cover Images:
https://stock.adobe.com/contributor/201135494/vera-kuttelvaserova?load_type=author&prev_url=detail

Printed and bound in the United States of America.

Contents

The Power of Love²

Prologue: Further Thoughts

I have written two books, and this will be my third. It completes the series of books I envisioned.

My first book, *Receiving the Gift We Give*, explored how to be a discerning and loving person while observing the larger world outside of ourselves.

My second book, *Essential Life Behaviours*, laid out a blueprint as to how we could become loving beings from within for ourselves and others.

This, my third book, *The Power of Love^2*, brings my first two books together by blending aspects of them into a continuing examination of love while discussing how we become higher beings.

I am a firm believer that love is energy and the driving, creative, and protective force within this universe. My definition of love includes joy. From my perspective, our universe includes all physical objects, life forms, dimensions, and various energy structures. Our universe holds more, but this list suffices.

Achieve to become a higher being through these ongoing goals:

1. Love the Universe, everyone, and everything in it.
2. Give gratitude for everything, including the good, bad, and indifferent.

3. Reject any notion of failure or unworthiness for yourself or others.
4. Recognise the necessity of lovingly expanding who you are.
5. Give yourself over to what brings you joy, feel it, and let your imagination and energy work for you.

Two commonalities unite every item on the above list. They each promote the energy of love outside of and within you, and they each have a unique energy feel.

Chapter 1: Belief Is Individual

We each hold our own spiritual beliefs, as we should.

Nonetheless, our spiritual beliefs may not be the same as another person's spiritual beliefs. This is also how it should be.

I have noticed many instances where individuals are strong in their spiritual beliefs. However, I've also observed instances where individuals are struggling with their spiritual beliefs.

Those who are strong in their spiritual beliefs often clash with others with strong, differing spiritual beliefs.

Although it is beneficial to hold strong spiritual beliefs, it is not constructive to consider spiritual beliefs that differ from yours as incorrect. These spiritual beliefs are personal and valid for the individuals who hold them. Declaring someone's spiritual beliefs as wrong often leads to hostility and undermines social harmony by fuelling anger, condemnation, and oppression.

This is not showing love, and when love is absent, it creates fear, hate, violence, and a collapse of human relations.

Understand that spiritual beliefs evolve through years of reflection, experiences, and feelings. Often, they are an integral part of who we are as individuals. Knowing the profound importance that many people place on their spiritual beliefs, it would be arrogant, unkind and disrespectful to dismiss another's spiritual beliefs as mistaken or inconsequential, especially to that person.

Similarly, crucial for humanity is to grasp the potential harm that can arise from abusing one's spiritual beliefs and to take measures to counteract it. In numerous families, communities, and cultures, individuals live in fear of expressing their genuinely differing spiritual beliefs due to threats of harassment, physical violence, and even death.

Asserting that someone's spiritual beliefs are incorrect and expressing this to them epitomizes ignorance. It also reflects a lack of self-esteem. Such behaviour neglects the importance of love, reality, comprehension, unity, and freedom for oneself and others.

A prime example that I have witnessed multiple times is the clash between theists and atheists. These individuals adhere to opposite beliefs. However, the question remains: which belief is the correct one?

Regrettably, there is ongoing debate about that question.

Spiritual beliefs are personal, and everyone is entitled to their own. Whenever you express your spiritual beliefs at any point in your life, they are valid for you. Right and wrong are subjective; what matters is what is correct for you at that moment. Telling another person why your spiritual beliefs are right and why their spiritual beliefs are wrong is a fool's errand. Nonetheless, I noticed that a lot of humanity has fallen into this foolishness.

Our spiritual beliefs are like our dietary preferences. Just as individuals and cultures have their preferred dishes, they also hold certain spiritual or other beliefs dear. However, as my brother once remarked in response to someone stating that the food they were eating was delicious, my brother said, "Yes it is, if you like it."

Most of us can acknowledge the wisdom in my brother's statement, given that we all possess our own preferred food dishes. The same understanding should be applied to our beliefs, regardless of whether we hold no spiritual beliefs or if our spiritual beliefs differ.

I want to talk about two belief systems: believers in deities and non-believers.

I profess my belief in God. However, I am not an adherent of any specific religion. Among the religions I've encountered, each one possesses elements of wisdom and love. Nonetheless, they also engage in practices that lead to harm through judgment, division, and an attitude of self-serving superiority.

As I consider belief to be individual, I will make no apologies for my spiritual beliefs, and no one else should make apologies for their spiritual beliefs. The God I believe in is Love, the Creator, and part of all Life. It is inconceivable for me to accept that God would have a favorite religion. We are all loved by God. A God who is the essence of Divine Love would not show favouritism, as it indicates a deficiency of love from God towards some of God's own children. After all, according to Judeo-Christianity, humanity was created in God's image. God, as the source of love, is incapable of not giving love. I have noticed that, for many people, their spiritual beliefs and behaviours contradict what I believe God is. This is also fine and as it should be. However, this behaviour often extends to ignoring their own Holy Texts, which is hypocritical.

There are individuals, atheists, who believe no deities exist. I have no issues with anyone who holds this as their belief. They have determined this based on their life experiences. I can't say I would believe differently if I experienced their life. This is the essence of deeply held beliefs. Throughout our lives, each of us develops our own set of spiritual beliefs. Individuals share their convictions and the reasons behind them, sometimes creating a collective synergy of spiritual beliefs. Therefore, a multitude of religions and belief systems exist. Similar to religious followers, atheists can get angry when others assert they are wrong.

It is imperative to broaden and enhance our understanding of personal spiritual opinions to encompass loving behaviours. The way we treat one another often inflicts harm. Whether through judgment, hatred, cruelty, division, degradation, or animosity, our actions can cause significant damage. Nevertheless, when discussing such harms, it seems appropriate to not just consider spiritual beliefs—which are opinions—and discuss the harms caused by other facets of our societies, including cultural, political, educational, wealth, status, or gender beliefs. When we weaponise our personal attributes, ignoring the well-being of others to boost our status, wealth, or ego, it reveals an entrenched absence of love. This lack of love hinders any society's growth, stopping it from achieving its true potential. We must end this harmful cycle, which we have perpetuated for far too long.

Nonetheless, there are two sides to our ego. One is what I term the harmful ego, driven by self-interest, manifesting when we abandon our love in favour of fear, intimidation, deceit, or a sense of superiority. Our love-based core values guide the other facet. For this side of our ego, we should feel uplifted by work achievements, accolades, and praise. This aspect of our ego understands such boosts can come from heartfelt interactions with others. Moments filled with love, praise, or recognition from a partner, friend, or family member often give us the most significant uplifts.

Love is the answer. Proclaiming that others' spiritual beliefs are incorrect generates anger, hatred, and animosity. At times, you may perceive others' spiritual beliefs as wrong, but in truth, they are only wrong for you. Trying to force sameness onto others fosters division and is a detriment to humanity.

Humanity will never be at peace, have joy, unity, or freedom until we understand this and behave appropriately with everyone with whom we interact.

Chapter 2: What Does Love Do?

To clarify, I consider love to be a form of energy that we show to the world that encompasses more than our families and sexual interactions with our partners.

Each of us shows we are coming from a space of love by eliminating our hate, anger, unworthiness, low self-esteem, fear, and related aspects and emotions. This includes various aspects and emotions, such as a desire to harm others due to envy, revenge, or vengeance, whether it's instigated by you, someone else, a group, or achieved through other means. This includes getting satisfaction when harm happens to someone. For example, when an accident occurs, and you delight in them being injured.

Nonetheless, people believe love can provoke fear, anger, or even abuse. We claim it underpins many of our actions. The intense love we have for someone or something can be overpowering. Many individuals go to great lengths to safeguard what they love— be it family, faith, principles, or their nation. For thousands of years, humans have battled over their loves. They attribute their jealousy, possessiveness, dependency, allegiance, or obsession to who or what they love. They defend their actions by claiming their love motivates them.

This form of love is not love, as it is restrictive and harmful. Comprehension of this opens our path to realising the wider significance of love. Love is the greatest powerful and creative force, fundamental to creation itself. It is limitless, elevating, and causes no harm.

Likewise, feelings of unworthiness and low self-esteem create negative emotions like hate, fear, and anger. Harbouring these feelings within yourself can restrict your energetic potential and hinder your ability to love. If you yearn for loving relationships, abundance, or the ability to make positive changes in your life, these negative emotions and beliefs will impede or prevent your progress. They act as barriers to love energy, which is the highest sustainable source of empowerment.

Once you accept your centre of love, the negativity from hate, anger, unworthiness, low self-esteem, and fear, along with their associated desires and feelings, cannot exist. Love has the power to energetically transform and remove them. Hate and anger are the opposite of love. Other examples of opposites are light and dark or wet and dry. One cannot exist within the other. They can exist side by side, but not in the same space. Nonetheless, you have the ability to cast your hate, fear, and anger into the energy field of love and have it transformed so it no longer has a hold on you. Making this happen is simpler than it seems. Here's what to do: envision a loving energy field encircling you or any place you choose. Actively sense and create a perpetual field of love for yourself. Acknowledge your feelings of hate, fear, or anger, and imagine them as part of your energetic essence. As these negative emotions arise within you, find their cause. Was it someone disrespecting you or a loved one, or did someone try to harm you or promote your harm? No matter the cause, you should expel the negative emotion. You can expel the negative emotion by calmly but explicitly releasing it from within you into your loving energy field. While doing so, express gratitude for its transformation and removal. You have the power to rid yourself of each facet of hate, fear, and anger.

Hate, anger, unworthiness, low self-esteem, fear, and their related wants and emotions cause you to be limited, boxed-in energetically, and less empowered to create your desires. Know that love does the opposite. Love is expansive and creative. Love opens your mind to a broader range of possibilities for succeeding. You become open to new opportunities and solutions. Love and joy can position you to obtain the goals that you desire. Love lets you consciously decide and take the actions that will create your avenues for success.

To be clear, this is personal success through our love. Without love, we create harmful paths to achieve success, which lead to our collapse and failure. Today, more than previously, those who gained power and success by harming others are now faltering and failing. When I examine the world today, I believe these failures are expanding.

Chapter 3: Energy

Quantum physics shows us, our world, our galaxy, and our universe is 99.999999% energy. The small remainder is matter. Our teachings often do not inform us that we are beings of energy.

Given that we are essentially composed of energy, it becomes clear that our abilities and influence should be primarily confined to this realm. Recognising this fundamental truth is crucial, as it empowers us to intentionally harness and direct energies for our own advantage. Everything in the universe has a distinct vibrational frequency, which means the wave speed is unique for differing items. As an example, the frequency of copper differs from the frequency of silver. Similarly, items with multiple materials produce a different frequency than each component material.

Your body and surrounding energy field have a vibrational frequency. An amazing aspect of our personal vibrational frequency is that it can change, and these changes can be measured. By studying people's vibrational frequencies, researchers discovered a correlation between a person's energy frequency and their emotional state. For example, anger and fear produce a much lower

The Power of Love^2

frequency than gratitude or love. We are able to consciously recognize frequencies as they change.

I will use love and anger energy as examples:

1. Love is wonderful and makes us joyous. People often describe love as feeling light, being happy, being on cloud nine, or blissful.
2. Anger makes us feel awful and unsettled. People describing anger often say they are annoyed, aggressive, enraged, or like a bull in a china shop. This is not being a happy, joyful person.

I was not going to explain our energies further. My question to most people would be, "Why don't you want to be happy?" It is our choice and decision not to be happy because we choose anger, fear, hate, or other lower-frequency energies. While certain ways of behaviour are taught to us under specific circumstances, we possess the ability to change our behaviours.

Energies differ from each other based on their vibrational frequencies. One way to picture this is by comparing it to sound or light. Each note of sound or each colour of light has a unique frequency. Yet, our senses are limited to only certain frequencies in the universe. Nonetheless, humanity has created devices to measure a wide range of vibrational frequencies.

It is important to understand how energy behaves. The universe is governed by energetic attraction. The phrase often used for this attraction is, 'like attracts like' (first attributed to the Greek philosopher Plato). A person's frequency will attract the same or similar frequencies from the universe. The energies will display an energetic attraction. Your love energy will attract love energy from the universe. Similarly, your anger energy will attract anger energy. This attraction applies to whatever energy you are putting out in the moment, whether it be gratitude, joy, love, despondency, fear, or scarcity.

I believe the most potent form of energy is love. By modifying our energy field to be one of love, the universe's energy responds in kind. Resulting in love allowing us to re-shape our reality. Regrettably, the majority of individuals are still to reach this loving state of consciousness. Nevertheless, it is within the reach of every individual to attain such a state. Albeit, most individuals have not been exposed to the consciously created expressions of love required for this realisation.

Whether or not we know it, our thoughts, words, and actions shape our love energies, with each more powerful than the last. This is how we create our reality. This is virtually what every person on Earth has done throughout their lives to create, albeit through their subconscious mind and ego. Our conscious mind and heart can create on a higher level. Interestingly, our negative and harmful behaviours block our love energy, which then hinders our ability to create. Otherwise, humanity would've been completely consumed by negativity a long time ago. This is why love shall prevail. Sadly, most people are not aware they are unconsciously creating their lives, both for good and ill.

Nevertheless, there are varying degrees of conscious love energy for creation. Often, it depends on how successful you are in envisioning and feeling the goal you desire and how completely loving and joyous you feel such an existence would be. Change your thoughts and words and attract the energy required to move forward.

Notice how successful people are driven to succeed. These people include researchers, entrepreneurs, professionals, artists, athletes, and more. Their strong vision encompasses their desires, emotions, and the significance their vision holds for them. I believe that joy is the signpost showing the way along our life's path. People take action and shift course along their path to follow their joy and ensure they succeed. What love energy does is expand your perspective, enabling you to discover new paths for success through innovative opportunities and solutions. Nevertheless, many individuals fail to succeed. They lose sight of the power of love due to misguided actions and behaviours. This frequently occurs due to missteps, impatience, and/or greed. Often, they abuse and misuse people, hoping to expedite their path to success. These harmful behaviours attract similar energies and create animosity in others, as well as revenge, and often lead to less success, no success, or criminal charges.

As an example, multiple studies show that building trust with your employees, clients, and customers will drive them to support your success. Trust has often been a key element in successful relationships, endeavours, leadership roles, and a company's success. As you may have suspected, trust is an expression of love.

Love should be the driving force behind your desired vision. Let your heart guide you in everything you do. Like trust, authenticity, competence, dedication, gratitude, and integrity, intertwine and are expressions of love. Embrace your passion and push forward, experiencing and feeling the joy of achieving your desires. Your joy will attract more joyous energies. Along this journey, share your vision with others and treat them with kindness, empathy, and respect. By doing so, you will become a leader who attracts loyal and passionate partners, employees, associates, friends, and clients. This is the ultimate recipe for success. Imagine having employees who express their love for their job, not only to you but to others as well. When you cultivate love within others, they will reciprocate it in numerous ways, including through dedication, creative thinking, imagination, and action.

Do not overlook my addition of friends and partners in the people listed above. These actions and behaviours are also beneficial in your closest relationships. Does anything hold greater importance than love and qualities like empathy, care, and nurturing in relationships?

However, do not be misled. Love incorporates critical thinking to achieve success, although I often assume it to be a part of competence. To achieve your goals, you must possess the necessary knowledge and wisdom to comprehend and appreciate any technical and practical aspects. Nevertheless, when you approach this endeavour with your heart and love, it will expand your ability to learn, create, and understand more fully the nuances of what is needed to succeed. Working with love energies leads to a better life.

Through love and its associated energies, we—as individuals and as humanity—will elevate ourselves to greater heights than ever before. There is an evolutionary shift approaching that will change who we are being. The days of concealed, self-serving agendas that cause immeasurable harm for the benefit of a few are coming to an end. We will propel our individual capabilities to levels previously only imagined. However, since these abilities must be grounded in love, humanity will aim for peace, understanding, unity, and freedom for everyone.

Chapter 4: Employing Critical Thinking and Understanding

In order to transform ourselves, it is crucial that we acknowledge our present state of being. To accomplish this, we need to understand what we observe and engage in critical thinking.

"Understanding" as a word and concept is multi-facetted. When I use the word "understanding", it means:

1. Knowledge about a subject, situation, person, group, etc., or how something works.
2. To obtain a clearer comprehension of the matters and individuals concerned.
3. Gaining awareness of one's own or another's abilities, disposition, emotions, apprehensions, or motives.
4. Releasing behaviors that cause harm to oneself or others.
5. You work diligently, with others, to develop love through intellectual integrity, humility, civility, empathy, appreciation, confidence, and trust.

The Power of Love[2]

To gain an unprejudiced comprehension of who you are requires "Critical Thinking". When I use "critical thinking" it means:

1. Make choices regarding sources of information and form your own viewpoint, emphasising a rational, objective, and self-aware approach.
2. Your ability to analyse information objectively can help you identify credible sources and strengthen your unprejudiced conclusions.
3. Your ability to remove negative motivations that are biased, selfish, manipulative, or otherwise create false or nonfactual conclusions.

The purpose of critical thinking and understanding is to free oneself from the limiting confines of one's own created false realities and harmful beliefs. This negative reality often hinders the full expression of love, including joy, unity, and freedom, which are aspects of love.

The process of removal often involves observing ourselves from an external perspective. We can attain this viewpoint either by self-reflection and/or through involving others. To examine our inner selves requires us to adopt a stance of self-observation. Observing ourselves is a deliberate mental action of stepping back from our beliefs, challenges, and emotions to view ourselves from an impartial standpoint. Imagine watching yourself in a movie you starred in and reflecting on your performance.

To enter this state of observation, find a comfortable seat, close your eyes, shift your mental focus inward, and find a place of stillness. Envision an empty space at the centre of your brain. Attain tranquillity by releasing your grip on external concerns, interruptions, and inquiries, allowing them to recede from your view. Recognise and distance yourself from external disturbances to immerse yourself into the serenity of the inner stillness of this space. Expanding your energy field to encompass love, joy, unity, and freedom enlarges you as a being by encompassing awareness, intuition, empathy, and creativity. Observe your behaviours in any situation and understand where and why your negative emotions overtook you. Feel into these moments and identify what triggered you. Use this understanding to prevent any future loss of self-control. Employ this same process to observe any instances where negative emotions controlled you. Ultimately, this moves us into a higher dimensional existence.

Embracing critical thinking and understanding combined with love can help us realise more fully our desires to expand and become greater than who we are now.

Chapter 5: Self Love Denied

Many of us have dealt with criticism, both justified and unjustified. Most criticism people receive is unjustified, based on what I've observed and heard. It is important to clarify that justified criticism must serve as a means of correction that will benefit a person. We use justified criticism when we observe that someone's actions demand harm to be caused, or by causing harm, to themselves or others, and they fail to recognize the negative consequences. Being harmful to others shows a lack of self-love. However, we should use our observational comments as an opportunity for growth and guidance rather than passing judgment. It is crucial to handle these situations with empathy and understanding to promote unity and enhance the individual's self-worth. Our actions should empower the person and help them develop a higher level of competence and confidence for the benefit of all.

People advocating harm for others are often being driven by fear. They believe their actions are justified because of a perceived threat to them or their loved ones. This is not the case, as they have latched onto the false fears created by others. The individuals promoting these false fears mainly do so to gain notoriety, fame, control, and money.

Regrettably, unwarranted criticism and promoting harm is just part of a larger problem. Alongside unwarranted criticism and hate, people engage in a range of harmful behaviours, such as physical and sexual abuse, exploitation, manipulation, cruelty, and neglect. These actions, whether experienced individually or in combination, add the potential to cause significant damage to the targeted individual, hindering their self-love and fostering low self-esteem.

If you were fortunate enough to grow up with great parents as I did, they spared you from unjustified criticism, especially during childhood. There are thousands of stories of parental abuse, whether that be physical, sexual, or emotional. Unfortunately, these types of parental abuse are rampant in all areas of our societies.

If you've faced parental abuse, remember, it's not and was not your fault. If your abuses were traumatising, I would recommend seeking professional counselling.

Parental abuse can be emotionally and mentally complicated and confusing. Repeated abuse of a child creates confusion and a lack of harmony. Children love their parents and recognize them as their source of food, shelter, comfort, treats, and presents. From birth, children develop a strong bond, especially with their mother and father. Children can become terror-ridden, horrified, and lost within any thoughts of their parents hating, physically harming, or abandoning them.

The Power of Love[2]

At three years old, I realised my parents could die in a car crash. It had never occurred to me that my parents would not be with me forever. The thought terrorised me for multiple weeks. Although nothing happened to my parents when I was a child, the thought of their death was enough to disrupt and change my worldview. When I remember what I went through, I cannot imagine how much more traumatised I could have been if my parents had said they hated me and/or threatened to abandon me.

Likewise, if we are told as children we are stupid, clumsy, incapable, ugly, fat, less than, and/or unwanted, with or without physical abuse, it will traumatise. I imagine if the continual hate and abuse continued into young adulthood, it would increase the traumatisation. Now imagine what effect constant abuse would have on a young child. Few things are less loving than child abuse.

Child abuse may instil feelings of unworthiness and guilt within a child. Such feelings can become ingrained and manifest in adulthood. They may surface often without conscious awareness. As parents, is this what you wish your children to attract energetically – unworthiness and guilt? Identifying these patterns of abuse is crucial, and seeking professional help to acknowledge and overcome them can be essential for healing.

Sadly, abuse lives not only in the domain of parenting. Siblings, relatives, teachers, friends, and other children can also be sources of abuse.

Often, we encounter bullies connected to our school and certain children. However, bullies can also associate with other bully friends or bullying relatives in the neighbourhood. These scenarios often include similar forms of abuse. Bullies accuse others of being stupid, clumsy, incapable, ugly, fat, less than, and/or unwanted. Again, with or without physical abuse. Nonetheless, physical abuse is common by such bullies.

From my understanding, bullies within schools often take on their parent's abuse habits, as it is a method of control and power the parents demonstrated as being normal or expected.

While abuse in our childhood can traumatise, so can abuse for adults. Take the abuses mentioned above and move them into adulthood. Common sources of abuse are from spouses, in-laws, friends, our family religion, cultural disagreements, the workplace, neighbours, and/or political beliefs.

When we consider the various forms of abuse that many of us experienced, witnessed, or heard, it becomes evident that mistreatment is rampant. Based on my understanding, sexual abuse affects twenty-five percent or more, a significant percentage, of children aged sixteen and under. The consequences of sexual abuse are profound and horrific for countless individuals. Often leading to their inability to love themselves or others. Regrettably, abuse inflicts trauma and instils recurring fears in individuals, too numerous for me to quantify here.

Suffering abuse does not make you guilty, unworthy, or inferior. If any of these resonate with you, it's vital to release these false beliefs and feelings. This is a key step in bolstering your self-love. Deep inside, most of you know who you are and recognize you are worthy of love. Ignore thoughts of being unworthy and ask yourself if there isn't a spark inside you saying otherwise. If you dream of worthiness and love but don't know how to obtain it, that spark is calling you. It is letting you know you are worthy of having love and self-love.

Numerous individuals are available to help you reach your destination, be they professionals or other caring people. Individuals who care do so because they've gone through similar abuses. Nonetheless, your journey toward self-love will be shaped uniquely by your personal circumstances. It is essential to first accept the belief that you are worthy of love. Combine your energy, critical thinking, understanding, and self-forgiveness to navigate your path toward your inner core of self-love. As your self-love grows, it will bring enhanced clarity and deep insights that were once hidden by your fears and feelings of inadequacy. Allow your inner light to dissolve away those clouds.

Chapter 6: Rebuilding Self Love

Babies and young children are innocent. Love fills our hearts for those nearby. Typically, they would be a parent or parents. Babies noisily inform us when they are uncomfortable, whether that is due to hunger, needing a diaper change, requiring sleep, playing with a toy, or wanting to be left alone. Upset babies are reacting to their feelings and physical state. Babies are direct, even when adults may not understand.

I have clear memories as a baby and a young child. While I acknowledge most people don't consciously retain such memories, I fortunately kept mine. Did I get upset as a baby from things I disliked or found uncomfortable? Yes, I did, as many babies do. Nevertheless, as I aged, I encountered a series of life-changing events that changed my worldview.

But how does this relate to self-love? The answer to this involves my memories of specific past events. Until age four, I believed I deserved and received love. It was a given. My parents provided it through my upbringing and our home. I loved my parents, siblings, relatives, neighbours, and I believed they loved me. Even when someone did something I considered bad, like taking my toy from me. I only cried because I wanted my toy back. It was straightforward and simple. I never thought it was due to a lack of love on anyone's part.

By the time I reached the age of five, I realized not everyone was loving. Upon starting kindergarten, that's when I witnessed the numerous cruel bullying actions towards others. Sometimes, I was the one being bullied, which left me confused. The behavior was incomprehensible to me and senseless. As I observed the damage inflicted on myself and others and recognised that such actions were inappropriate. They were harmful and pointless. Despite the bullies' cruelty, I never considered their behavior to be my fault. Sadly, I saw children bullied, and they couldn't understand why and what they did wrong and blamed themselves. In my view, the individuals subjected to bullying are blameless. Often, they were the quieter, reserved, gentler, and kinder children. A few years later, I understood these qualities made them targets for bullies who discovered this type of person wouldn't retaliate, giving the bullies a sense of power without facing any serious consequences.

I didn't realize until I was eight years old that the cruel behavior of these children was largely influenced by their parents. I understood their behaviour when I realised how abused they were at home.

A neighbour, a girl named Susan (fake name), was cruel to me by doing harmful things to me when around her. This escalated until, one day, she moved far beyond her normal cruelty. While playing at her house, she mentioned having a task to complete for her father before his return from work. She asked me if I could help her. I said yes. She led me to their garage and informed me that the large bottles at the back needed to be emptied into the garden. I saw around thirty large bottles stacked up. I asked her why, but she didn't know. However, she stated that those were the instructions her father had given her. She dragged one bottle out and emptied it into the garden. The bottles contained a clear liquid with no smell, so I thought it must be old water. After I helped her empty the bottles, she thanked me and said her parents would be home soon to make dinner. So I left to go back home.

A couple of hours later, we heard a loud banging at our front door, and it was Susan's father. He yelled at my parents and looked furious. He told them I had emptied a poisonous chemical into their garden. He added that Susan had told him she was unable to prevent me from emptying the bottles, and he viewed my actions as inexcusable. After he left, I explained what happened to my parents, but they did not say a word.

The next morning, Susan's mother came to our house and threatened that if her prized climbing rose died, she would hold my parents responsible for the cost of replacement. Sadly, I loved that climbing rose as it covered the entire side of their house, and it was a glory to see it bloom thousands of flowers every year. I prayed no harm came to it. Luckily, it never died or got harmed.

Because of my anger towards Susan, I decided to confront her. I knocked on her front door, and Susan opened the door. When I asked her why she lied about what happened, her father grabbed her, pushed her back, and yelled at me. He asked me how I dare blame his daughter, who is a good girl and who has never done anything wrong. According to him, she was his "perfect little princess", so how could I attack her with such lies? He further stated this proved me a monster and told me to get off his property or he would call the police. He instructed me to never approach his daughter or come onto his property again. Then forcefully closed the door.

Strangely enough, I used to consider Susan a close friend, and she even expressed the same sentiment towards me. However, my perception of her changed drastically when I stumbled upon these unsettling truths. Reflecting on the events that transpired, it became clear to me that some individuals may suffer from mental imbalances. Did this incident cause me pain? Yes, it did. As a result, I never had the opportunity to see Susan again. Nevertheless, this occurrence shed light on a few crucial aspects regarding those involved. First, I realised it is vital to exercise caution when dealing with people, regardless of their outward kindness or claims of friendship. Second, there had been past signs by her dishonesty that I had previously overlooked because of our friendship. Third, Susan's parents harboured delusions about their daughter, blindly believing her every word and considering her incapable of any wrongdoing. Fourth, Susan herself displayed a cruel and imbalanced nature, undoubtedly influenced by the way her parents spoiled her, allowing her to fabricate lies and escape the consequences of her malicious actions. Last, I realised Susan possessed a devious side, as this elaborate scheme would not have unfolded without careful premeditation on her part.

The Power of Love[2]

From that moment onward, whenever Susan's father saw me, he yelled various insults at me, even across the street. He'd shout, "You're a snake in the grass", and other nasty statements. This continued for many years. It made me sad, and I felt sorry for him, as he was being misguided. I wanted to show him the truth, but I knew that would not happen. Still, I never let Susan's or her parent's actions lower my self-esteem or hinder my self-love. It wasn't until later in life that I realized my decisions had led me to attract energies of self-esteem and self-love. After those events, my parents never said a word to me, as they recognised I spoke the truth. Somehow, they always did, and they avoided Susan and her family.

I could tell you more cruel experiences from school bullies, including teachers, to psychotic friends and neighbourhood gangs. I decided to never allow the cruelty to bother me unless it became violent towards me or others. Then, my self-preservation kicked in. I took to heart the phrase, "Sticks and stones may break my bones, but words will never hurt me." The phrase resonated with me as it highlighted the connection between cruel behaviour and a lack of nurturing relationships.

Every time I watched the behaviours of these cruel individuals, I tried to explore their relationships to understand how others had treated them. Often, I found their treatment from their parents or siblings either demanding, demeaning, verbally abusive, and/or physically abusive. Because of their treatment, I understood why these cruel individuals became abusive. I understood that many children lashed out when away from their homes to relieve stress

27

and/or to mimic their parents. I believe they did this to feel more powerful and to prove their worth as a person. Their parents, siblings, and sometimes others became their role models for not feeling powerless. I realised cruel words would never hurt me as they held no truth. Likewise, I vowed I would not allow abuse in any form to change me from who I knew I should be, or so I thought. This decision did open me up to the universal energies of integrity and self-worth.

We need to acknowledge the cruel words and abuse from imbalanced and mistreated individuals and recognise they hold no truth. It's important to remember that you are being targeted to cause you pain and emotional distress. Don't let either of them affect who you are because you might start doubting yourself and follow the abuser's way of life. Realising this has empowered me to continue nurturing my self-esteem and self-love and to attract more energies of the same. However, on a personal level, it saddens me to observe the harm caused by the abuse to and from young people. I understood that a child's self-love was being diminished due to cruelty from external sources, which they couldn't fully grasp or handle properly. As the abuse persists, the personal trauma intensifies, especially for children whose distorted environment is created by the very people they love and trust, such as parents, friends, teachers, coaches, or clergy.

When able, as parents, neighbours, or friends, we should notice such abusive behaviours and bring our love and understanding to those in need. A good application includes counsellors, outreach personnel, or a caring friend who listens and cares.

The abusive situations I experienced, as related above, turned out to be positive learning lessons for me. It is important that what we regard as a negative event has a silver lining. Through discovery and understanding, we gain awareness of people's behaviour and its reasons. Stay observant, understanding, and free from anger or retribution to raise your energy.

Beyond the abuse events, positive events also occur, which change our lives. I shall provide two examples of what I experienced as a child. When I was a baby, my mother bathed me in the kitchen sink, but one day, my father took on this task. I lacked time awareness, but now I realise I was less than a year old. While being bathed, my father talked to me, unlike my mother. Her words were few and intermittent, unlike my father's constant chatter.

It was surprising to find that I could understand some of my father's words. I could not speak, at least to my satisfaction, so I listened. This was when I realised I could understand simple statements. It was the first time I consciously realized this; although I recall grasping some previous words, this particular moment marked my first conscious recognition of understanding someone's statements to me. From that point forward, I listened to people to comprehend what they said to me or others. However, I refrained from speaking until I became confident in my ability to have such conversations. I remember being frustrated that I could not understand all the words being said. My not talking caused my parents distress, that is, until I turned three and started speaking.

Then, for a year, I never stopped speaking. I remember at one point the doctor telling my parents I was fine and I would speak when ready.

Nevertheless, another moment during that bath gave me a second world-changing insight. It occurred when my father put me in the water. As soon as he did, I screamed. My father felt the water and then pushed the faucet away. He realised the faucet was hot to the touch. He apologised to me and stated it was because my back touched the hot faucet.

This astonished me. I understood his words and, for the first time, recognized that the world around me had a direct impact on me. The heat from the faucet caused discomfort in my back, and it was a revelation that transformed my life. With time, I realised my limited understanding of the world made it difficult to differentiate between what was harmful and what was not. One particular incident stands out from when I was four years old: I stuck my finger in a candle's flame during dinner. Although I didn't suffer any serious burns, it was undeniably painful. This served as an important life lesson on the perils of fire. I had numerous other similar learning experiences, but I won't delve into any more of them.

The experiences of abuse have taught me about potential pitfalls and their underlying causes, enabling me to work on solutions from my heart and love. They have sharpened my observation skills, heightened my awareness, and deepened my understanding. My positive experiences have allowed me to feel and witness their occurrence, revealing their profound impact.

The Power of Love[2]

Both abusive and positive experiences equip us with the inner strength necessary to steer our personal growth that will occur through our love energy and its attraction to us.

Chapter 7: Our Children

How can we bring love and freedom to humanity? I believe the answer lies with our children.

An effective way to create lasting change in society is by educating our children. By explaining the interconnectedness of life and the importance of unity through examples, we impart this wisdom to the forthcoming generations. However, this ideal is not our current reality. The root of humanity's discord lies in our lack of awareness and understanding. While reading, writing, and arithmetic are touted as the pillars of our children's education, they should only be one aspect of education. What's missing is what I term the three Rs: Rights, Respect, and Responsibility. Our children should learn that every person deserves love, joy, unity, understanding, and freedom, regardless of race, nationality, education, religion, social status, gender, sexual orientation, or beliefs. They need to develop a deep understanding about love and societal behaviour, focusing on rights, respect, and responsibilities, beginning in preschool and continuing through high school.

Rights

Our children must learn equality in rights for all people. A CEO's rights should not outweigh a file clerk, nor should a president surpass a homemaker under the law. While the law proclaims equal rights for all, we know this is not true. Often, those with wealth, power, or celebrity status receive preferential treatment because of who they are or by hiring the best lawyers. Likewise, prejudice plays a significant role in this disparity. It is not, nor has it ever been, a level playing field.

Our discrimination, both overt and subtle, that occurs in every town, city, county, or country must end. We must educate our children on the significance of equal rights and help them recognize societal prejudices. They should learn to address these issues lovingly and purposefully, setting an example for others and reinforcing this awareness in their hearts. Our children need to see that we are One, and our actions affect all of us. We must have an open dialogue about rights issues with our children, including the challenges they will encounter both at home and in the wider world, in order to promote the rights of everyone.

Educating our children on these matters encourages them to naturally bring unity, understanding, and freedom into everyone's lives. This education, as they carry it into adulthood, will inspire them—as future CEOs, manufacturers, politicians, engineers, scientists, and service providers—to take pride and joy in ensuring people's rights.

Respect

Everyone should treat others as they themselves would like to be treated. This concept sounds simple enough, yet it is often challenging because individuals can be self-absorbed.

Demonstrating everyday courtesy and manners are signs of respect. Control over one's temper and not lashing out in anger is also a form of respect. It is important for our children to recognize that while anger is a natural emotion, having compassion and empathy is more respectful and will win out over anger. People show disrespect for many reasons. From my observations, the major causes include stress, low self-esteem, depression, anger, fear, and prejudice, all of which are because of a lack of understanding and the awareness of oneness.

Just like rights, individuals with wealth, authority, or fame deserve no more respect than the general population, yet society conditions us to hold prominent figures in higher regard. However, with modern communications and extensive information sharing, we now understand that influential individuals have not earned such admiration but have influenced it based on their material wealth and popularity. When we hold prominent individuals accountable for their reckless actions, it shows that they are human, just like everyone else.

Society has conditioned us to perceive certain individuals as superior to those less fortunate. How would you react if made to feel inferior due to your background, financial, or social status? When we look down on certain people, do we expect gratitude? How would you respond if someone treated you as less than human based on who you are? It is my belief that such ongoing mistreatment leads to retaliation. I am not surprised by these behaviours, based on my observations.

Unloving behaviours cause unloving reactions.

The Power of Love[2]

Our children need to be taught how to interact with others regardless of our differences so they understand how being respected feels. We have a multitude of real-life scenarios to use as teaching tools. It is only through understanding various personal perspectives that our children will respect and honour humankind.

Responsibility

It is crucial for our children to understand that their actions and words have consequences, leading to either positive change or harm in the world. Additionally, we must teach them that our responsibilities extend beyond humanity to all the life forms we encounter during our lives. Teach children about the interconnectedness of life and the impact of actions on others and themselves. We can do this by fostering critical thinking and understanding.

It is common to categorise responsibility into sub-categories that include social, individual, corporate, legal, ministerial, or moral. The impression I have is that we're over-analysing responsibility. In my opinion, there is only one type of responsibility: individual responsibility. I define responsibility as taking personal accountability and working to make sure others take accountability to ensure love, joy, unity, understanding, and freedom are present in everyone's lives. It is difficult to grasp why social, individual, corporate, legal, ministerial, or moral spheres of responsibility would not encompass love, joy, unity, understanding, and freedom, especially when applying critical thinking. I believe we divide areas of responsibility in a way that often results in people with wealth and/or authority having fewer responsibilities.

Our love from the heart will serve individuals, corporations, governments, religions, and other institutions or groups. I believe corporate social responsibility (known as corporate conscience), where self-imposed regulations outline a corporation's responsibilities to preserve the welfare and interests of the organisation and society, has sidetracked us. While I don't disagree, everyone, including CEOs, management, employees, stockholders, and board members, must take personal responsibility to make sure love, joy, unity, understanding, and freedom are present in everyone's lives.

Rights, Respect, and Responsibility Unified

Western society promotes the right to freedom, yet the act of interfering with freedom remains widespread. Talk about providing a mixed message! Prejudice, self-righteousness, and greed are driven by fear, and through our own lack of self-esteem and an overblown sense of self-importance. Fear controls us when we lose our connection with love, leading to the abuse and manipulation of others for personal gain. By embracing our heart and love, we teach our children the true meaning of rights, respect, and responsibility.

Be forewarned; we should be prepared to stand back from our egos once we enlighten our children. As our children will point out the thousands of things we should change to create the better world we keep talking about. In this way, we may begin to remove the endless cycle of strife in our world and prevent our children from inheriting it. Our children will then have the clearest insights, and we must allow them the freedom to use them.

Once children take ownership of the complete spectrum of the three Rs, they will reach adulthood prepared to implement the three Rs into every aspect of their lives, whether personal or work-related. They will leave no human endeavour untouched. Their understanding and knowing that we are One will ensure that love, joy, unity, understanding, and freedom are in our lives. Educating our children on the meanings of rights, respect, and responsibility provides future generations with a new foundation, enabling everyone to have positive, loving interactions on a social, individual, work, and environmental basis.

Chapter 8: Self Love as Adults

To love someone else, you must first love oneself. If love is not within you, you cannot extend it to others. A lack of self-love, or even experiencing self-hatred, can result in feelings of being unworthy of love from others.

No one needs a specific person, as the essence of who we are is already in our core of love. Creating a centre of neediness is detrimental and benefits no one. Reflect on your current or past relationships. Do these relationships make you feel incomplete or lost without them over time? Consider your response carefully and honestly. It's a challenging question that may stir emotions. Experiencing sadness after the end of a relationship is a natural response. Trying to get them back by saying you need them is not. If you claim you need them, it shows a lack of self-love and a potential lifelong quest to find fulfilment in others rather than within yourself. This creates an emotional detachment from your heart and is increasingly harmful the longer it lasts. Love is not needy.

Likewise, our self-love and worthiness face assault during childhood and thereafter. As adults, we may encounter a whole new realm of abuse and cruelty, which can hinder our self-love and create beliefs of being unworthy, thereby lowering our self-esteem.

Below is a short list of specific statements or actions that create unworthiness, which we can face as adults. To be clear, some individuals are still subjected to childhood abuse.

Here are some common abusive statements:

1. Your high school, college, or university grades are not good enough.
2. If you can't do this, then you are not a man.
3. You are just a woman.
4. I find it repulsive that you, someone from that culture, would have the nerve to disagree with me.
5. You are a faggot; you are a dyke.
6. It is your duty as my wife to obey everything I say.
7. I wanted a boy - why did you give birth to a useless girl?
8. If you can't understand your job, then maybe you deserve to be fired.
9. I am your boss, and you will do everything I say, understand?
10. You are a disappointment as our child.
11. You may be an adult, but I am your parent, and you shall do as I say.
12. Our family will disown you if you don't follow the family religion.
13. You do not make enough money - you are useless.
14. Your wants don't matter - I am more important.
15. Yes, I took credit for your work, live and learn, sucker.
16. Public humiliation by a boss, co-workers, teachers, or friends.

The Power of Love[2]

The list above is not complete. I observed them all being said, just from memory. From this list, it shows that abuse in childhood does not disappear when you become an adult. Abuse can still take place by your parents and siblings. Nonetheless, as an adult, you witness new forms of abuse not experienced in childhood. Examples could include abuse from partners, professors, friends, coworkers, or bosses. I am sure in reading this list you could add to it from your experiences.

We lose whenever someone puts another person down, abuses them, or vilifies them. Each such occurrence makes our world less developed, unstable, and/or less peaceful. This makes our societies less safe.

Fortunately, adults of any age can remove their abusive behaviours. It is their choice. You can make this choice at any time. Acknowledging the harm caused by abuse and deciding to change is a positive first step. However, there is no definitive right or wrong for anyone or any situation. The important thing is to remove abusive behaviour. It doesn't matter if you are the giver or receiver of abuse. It's crucial to address abuse as the giver, but so is removing yourself from the abuse and its related emotional impacts.

Educating individuals to remove the emotional impact of abuse as recipients can help eradicate abuse. Remember, a person's move to a higher frequency by removing abuse, such as to happiness from fear, attracts similar energies. Staying in a state of fear just attracts fear. Nonetheless, recognising that abuse reflects the abuser's psychological issues rather than our own can prevent us from becoming abusers. This understanding can help, at least partially, to eliminate abuse within our families, friendships, and workplaces. Nonetheless, some individuals will persist in their abusive behaviour regardless of our actions. If all other strategies fail, distancing oneself from the abuser may sometimes be the best course of action.

Numerous stories depict children recognising parental abuse as they mature into adulthood. Regardless of how you explain to your abusers their behaviours and your feelings, many abusers will remain unchanged. Sometimes severing ties is the best course of action. This may lead parents to acknowledge their errors and transform, or at the very least, it can provide the abused with less stress and a happier life. Ending contact isn't limited to parental relationships. Regrettably, sometimes this may entail switching jobs or pursuing a divorce. Can you envision a life free from abuse? Would happiness and liberation resurface after a prolonged absence of mistreatment? Could you rediscover yourself and find contentment? Determine your path forward by assessing the impact on your life and well-being with others' assistance. Fortunately, many people and organisations are available to help escape abusive situations.

Regardless of age, we can instinctively identify abusers. Most often, we admire, respect, and trust a kind, nonabusive person versus an abusive one. We often do this, whether consciously or not. Likewise, we can emulate people we admire, respect, and trust. Which, when done, leads us to increase our self-love and strengthen our level of self esteem.

The Power of Love[2]

It's incredible how love, in all its forms, can transform our world, both within and around us.

Chapter 9: Self Love and Beliefs

Our personal beliefs, whether religious or otherwise, spark intense discussions. Arguments over our beliefs lead to many disagreements, animosity, and self-righteous behaviours.

Though beliefs are personal, some individuals tend to shift from self-love to self-aggrandisement. I have often witnessed people labelling others as evil, worthless, or destined for Hell because of their beliefs. This is because these individuals hold the view that their personal beliefs should apply to others.

What makes these situations worse is the people spouting such judgements often associate with a group of similar beliefs. The herd mentality is often led by specific individuals who propagate this self-aggrandisement. I have seen this in multiple religions. Still, to be fair, I have also seen many religious groups that oppose this brainwashing and the resultant behaviours. Unfortunately, as a well-known saying intones, the squeaky wheel gets the attention.

Self-love and self-esteem are intertwined and can affect one another. I believe and assert that low self-esteem is a fundamental underlying factor behind numerous detrimental behaviours. Those with low self-esteem experience a significant surge in ego and confidence when praised, feel superior to others, or achieve personal milestones. This can indeed be a positive occurrence, as long as these instances do not inflate their ego unrealistically, resulting in creating negative behaviours.

Nevertheless, many people recognize this cause and effect and use it to feed off of and control others. They use it to gain personal fame, power, and wealth. This applies to multiple religious, political, intellectual, and societal groups. Societies globally have formed hierarchical divisions where certain groups consider themselves superior to others.

All of us have experienced the disapproval of others, either through claims of superiority or the constant reminder of our supposed inferiority. I will focus on one group for illustration without lengthy explanations from multiple examples. As I live in North America, where Christianity is the dominant religion, Christianity is a suitable topic of discussion.

Certain Christian groups often ignore the primary themes of Christianity's Holy Books to promote judgement, hate, and superiority and to control individuals with low self-love and low self-esteem. To be clear, these Christian churches likely represent less than twenty percent of churches in North America. Nevertheless, they wield immense influence within their communities and attract significant media coverage. Some promote their beliefs through televised sermons. They achieve group self-aggrandisement by convincing individuals they know better than much of the population or sometimes other Christians.

By asserting that they have superior knowledge of God compared with others, they cultivate a sense of superiority within their group. They further reinforce this notion by claiming to have a close relationship with God and a deeper understanding of God's desires. They reinforce the message's superiority by attributing it to the Creator and Ultimate being. In doing so, they have constructed a lofty pedestal for themselves from which they proclaim their superiority.

What such groups seem to not recognize is that creating separation, judgement, and superiority sews deep division, a lack of love, heart, or understanding. Christianity sometimes diverges from Jesus' teachings. For example, when asked, Jesus stated two overriding commandments. I shall only mention the second one, which states, "Love your neighbour as yourself", and then Jesus stated, "These two commandments encompass all the law and prophets." (Mark 12:29-31, KJV).

Is there love and heart in elevating oneself onto a pedestal, being judgemental, and claiming superiority over others because of a stated closeness to God? This behaviour shows no love for your neighbours, except for the select few who agree. I understand why some Christian groups, or any groups, including political groups, do this. It is to gain influence, power, and wealth. Regardless, for specific Christian groups, ignoring specific major parts of Jesus' teachings so they can gain influence, power, and wealth tells us who they are, which is misguided and hypocritical.

These behaviours can not build self-love. Self aggrandisement based on judgement and false superiority is a bloated ego play.

Likewise, the large ego hides their low self-esteem. And they keep attracting and reinforcing those same low-frequency energies through their behaviours. Notice how many people find it difficult to change their negative behaviours, no matter what you explain to them? It is because they are in a negative energy loop where like energy attracts like energy.

Still, love is the answer.

Although some religious groups receive media attention for their lack of love, there are many others that are driven by love. The problem is that their message doesn't grab attention, and the media don't consider it sensational enough to mention. But this is not what should happen. Promoting love, compassion, empathy, understanding, and acceptance of others is far more spectacular than unloving behaviours. We should demand better.

Following a path of loving your neighbour is a monumental behavioural change that would help humanity. It could eradicate crime, poverty, hate, judgement, and the superiority complexes we believe. What could be more sensational? Yet, some individuals ignore the message of loving one's neighbor in order to feel superior. But, in reality, they have created a false paradigm. People box themselves into a belief that their actions are for the greater good. This becomes false when people vilify and call for eradicating others because of differing beliefs, regardless of the topic and people targeted. There is no love in this behaviour.

Love does not choose, and love has no boundaries or restrictions. Most of us have been taught that we should think, show, and display love in a hierarchical pyramid arrangement, where we place ourselves or God at the top. Below God/self, we find immediate family members, then friends, and then pets. Typically, there are layers of people in the middle of this pyramid, including other family members, co-workers, neighbours, employees, religious groups, political groups, cultural groups, and sometimes animals and plant life. In this pyramidal arrangement, we place those we show the least love towards at the bottom. The lower categories, including the destitute, those we hold prejudices against, and unfamiliar individuals, are often disregarded as unimportant.

As a person who believes love is the answer, I believe it is not wrong to point out unloving behaviours, regardless of religion, politics, wealth, or educational affiliation, where I define an unloving behaviour as being an action or inaction that causes harm to others, whether that harm is physical, emotional, infringing on freedoms, or financial.

Nonetheless, how can we bring about change without provoking anger in others? The answer is quite simple. We must approach the matter with love and sincerity. By setting a positive example through our behaviour, actions, and communication, we can inspire others to follow our lead. Our energy fields interact, so it is important to consciously not let a person's lower frequency field to overtake yours. Likewise, recognize that your higher frequency energy field will be affecting the other person's energy field. To achieve this, we must remain steadfast in our love, empathy, and compassion, and ensure that our thoughts, words, and actions are in harmony with these values. It is essential to keep your vibrational frequency high. Likewise, it is important to engage in active listening, partake in meaningful conversations, and demonstrate empathy and affection. Will everyone embrace this change? Probably not. In the future, social pressure will increase and encourage people to embrace the wisdom of love.

Chapter 10: Love is the Answer

Many of you will recognize the negative scenarios I have outlined above in relation to creating low self-esteem and a lack of self-love. When you read them, I imagine they bring back negative experiences for you. Some will add a layer of guilt, regret, hurt, or anger towards certain people.

These each hinder you and your ability to love. Recognise and release lower vibrational negative emotions such as guilt, regret, hurt, and anger to further unlock your long-term potential.

Let your self hindrances go and come from love and your heart. This applies to each of us. While being hobbled by your guilt, regret, hurt, or anger, do you believe you can show competence, acceptance, respect, empathy, integrity, trust, unity, or wisdom? You may believe you do, but you do not. Progressing towards a healthier state of being is the best goal.

As my father always told me, "Worrying solves nothing. All it does is cause unneeded stress. Let your worries go." The same wisdom applies to guilt, regret, hurt, and anger. Let them go. Sadly, I forgot what my childhood years taught me and succumbed to these emotions. As a teenager, I used to get manipulated by my guilt, regret, hurt, anger, and worry. When I caused harm to someone, it would eventually devastate me. Whether anger or a need for revenge pushed my actions, causing harm, my guilt over my harmful actions was not strong enough to release me from my hate or vengeful thoughts. My ego found satisfaction in these harmful actions for a short time, but my anger never totally dissipated. I'd stay angry, regardless of the time that had passed. It took a few years to realise the harm I was causing myself, as my lessons from childhood reminded me.

Likewise, when someone made me guilty for who I was, I knew inside the person belittling me was incorrect. Nonetheless, with each recurrence, guilt and self-doubt grew within me. One example involved sports. Particularly football, baseball or similar team sports. I was horrible at them, and no matter how hard I tried, I could not improve. However, late in high school, I discovered I had a disability. Oddly, I couldn't run and catch a ball simultaneously. When I was running to catch a ball, as I put my arms in motion to catch the ball, my feet would stop, and I would fall. I don't know the full explanation, but a doctor told me my right and left-brain connection would become overloaded, and I could only do one of these things at a time.

After I endured years of ridicule and being chosen last for teams, I felt worthless, unneeded, ashamed, and guilty. Once I realised my inability, I quit participating in those sports. I let go of my guilt, shame, and hurt that I accepted into myself from others. Nevertheless, there was a silver lining. I discovered my talents and broke free from others' perceptions. I found I had excellent eye-hand coordination and used them to perform intricate jobs. My mind, capable despite my body, turned to writing, reading, art, public speaking, and more. This focus and shift came in handy as I progressed through university and into various jobs. It was then that I understood I needed to let go of my anger from my teenage years.

This experience taught me to love myself for what I was able to do because I developed my talents around what I loved. It caused me to know individuals are gifted and unique. As I observed the people around me, I realised that some become known for their talents. Their commonality was their love for their work. I observe that schools often push specific talents as being of the highest importance onto students. This still applies to sports in some schools today. If a sport is your talent and you enjoy it, then I agree: throw yourself into doing your best. Nonetheless, it is harmful and abusive to put others down because their talents lie elsewhere. Demeaning students because they want to be athletes, computer nerds, artists, mathematicians or whatever, does a disservice to all of them. Whether by parents, students, or teachers, behaving in this manner hinders people from becoming who they desire to be.

Sadly, a significant number of people do not love their jobs. Failing to utilise their inherent talents may lead to this situation, and those around them can exacerbate it. When someone does not love their job, there is a lack of love, whether from others or yourself.

Regrettably, in a vast majority of jobs, coworkers and leaders do not work with their fellow employees to help them improve. Love compels you to lend a hand to your fellow employees, whether it's enhancing their work or guiding them toward a better-suited job. Often, employees avoid asking for help as they fear it might be perceived as a sign of weakness. I have worked in companies that foster this atmosphere. This resulted in numerous blunders, causing financial and time losses that stemmed from incompetence and the reluctance to seek help.

Similarly, helping others to become better at what they do applies to students, parents, siblings, and friends. It is not just limited to our work environment. Nonetheless, I think our workplaces are the most appalling examples for many people.

Approaching people from a place of love and your heart will resolve these issues. Love is that powerful.

When your behaviour embraces competence, confidence, acceptance, respect, empathy, integrity, independence, trust, unity, and/or wisdom, it shows you have self-love and self-esteem. It is by embracing these behaviours that you can cultivate a presence of love. That is why I sometimes call these the "Essential Life Behaviours".

Chapter 11: Abundance

Do you find yourself blocked from having abundance, including money and good relationships? The behaviours of love will assist you in removing these blockages. Often, individuals self-create and/or self-perpetuate these blockages, with the culprits being limited beliefs, wants, and false expectations. Naturally, competence and confidence can help build self-love and improve your self-esteem. This often leads to better finances and the possibility of improved relationships. Nonetheless, acceptance is one of the major keys to abundance and good relationships. From a financial perspective, when people are in a state of lacking something, whether money or possessions, they focus on everything they want. They state they want money, trips, cars, better clothes, a better residence, and many other things. They continually complain about what they "want" or "need". Remember, thoughts, words, and actions have the power to create. Your words tell the universe who you are and exactly what you are asking. If you say that you "want" something, the energies will respond by granting your "wanting" that item. Why? Because that is the energy you are putting out to the universe and is what you requested. If you stated, "I want a new car!" the universe responds by saying, "Yes, you do want a new car" and gives you more "want" energy.

Would it not be better to say what you mean? Use the words "get", "receive", or "have" instead of "want" or "need" - whichever suits your request. Love expressed is not needy. It is clear and precise about your feelings and what you desire for yourself or others. Is it the energy of "getting, receiving, having" that you desire, rather than the energy of "wanting or needing"?

Then, release and embrace your current situation. Accept what you do not have at the moment and move into your heart and love. Remember, love expands your perspective, enabling you to discover new paths to success through innovative opportunities and solutions. Do not believe you are inadequate because you lack funds for luxury items. If you emit energy that states your lack, want, or you are unworthy, that is what will be reinforced back to you. Acknowledging your current state doesn't imply accepting your future state. Look to the future and create a vision of your future life. Create what you envision, feel it, and give thanks for those goals. "Want" or "need" continues to foster low self-esteem and shows no self-love.

While I have emphasised the significance of these behaviours in work and personal home environment, they apply to relatives, friendships, neighbours, and anyone else you encounter. Additionally, I will include the behaviours of acceptance, authenticity, gratitude, awareness, honesty, humility, responsibility, courage, observation, and grace. By incorporating some or all of these behaviours into your life or the lives of others, your love brings joy, understanding, unity, and freedom. By exuding these, you will attract them back to you. Whether the impact is minor or life-changing, these moments hold immense importance. Remember, assisting someone and then witnessing a transformation in their life for the better is extremely fulfilling. Even the smallest seed planted can become something extraordinary; never underestimate your potential. Every loving action will bring that energy to you.

Without love, it is impossible to accomplish these things. Although individuals may still overlook this assertion, can anyone genuinely believe that arrogance, condescension, disrespect, lack of empathy, or judgmental behaviour will truly lead to happiness, build trust, or garner respect from others? Even removing the universal energy considerations this is just common sense from our observations of people.

Chapter 12: The Foundation of Love Energy

Love is the utmost powerful energy force in the universe, and its power is endless. Before you can embrace the power of love, you must first become a loving being. It is simple in concept. If you wish to utilise this love energy, you must attract love energy.

As discussed, negative energy that is permeated by hate, anger, revenge, superiority, judgment, control of others, or similar harmful behaviours in any form, does not attract love energy. Love energy is attracted by:

1. Embracing self-love.
2. Knowing you are worthy is starting to remove your low self-esteem.
3. Changing your behaviours by embracing competence, confidence, acceptance, respect, empathy, integrity, independence, trust, unity, and/or wisdom.
4. Likewise, we must become beings of acceptance, authenticity, gratitude, awareness, honesty, humility, responsibility, courage, observation, and grace.

The Power of Love[2]

Realise that love doesn't demand you fully transform before its power emerges into your life.

Expanding as loving individuals brings benefits with each step. Gradually your hate, anger, worries, unworthiness, low self esteem, and fears will fade. Your mind will open up to a broader range of possibilities, new opportunities, and solutions for your problems, and you will be better able to create a path to your highest goals and desires.

Nonetheless, it must be paramount in who we are being that your love has the following foundational parts:

1. Cause no harm to others, whether directly or indirectly. Your love would not allow you to harm yourself or other people. Similarly, your love would not permit you to allow indirect harm to come to others.
2. Maintain a positive mindset and express gratitude for what you have and your surroundings. Studies have shown that having a positive mindset paired with gratitude improves memory, work efficiency, and increases by up to twenty percent our thinking ability.
3. Love always guides you towards something better in life. When we experience the death of a loved one or any shocking situation, we cannot avoid grief. However, if you have striven to be loving, you will become resilient. Additionally, you will attract people who will offer you the support and love you require.

Chapter 13: What is Next?

As we embrace love, who we are becoming will affect those people around us. As you become an ever-increasing beacon of light through your love, you will cast your and other people's shadows aside. Sadly, those who refuse to leave the shadows may develop hatred towards those who embody love. I appreciate a particular biblical statement that conveys the following sentiment, which I will rephrase: 'As the light gets brighter, the shadows become darker.'

Regardless of the circumstances, love is an undeniable force. Your love's brightness and expansion will inspire others to love. Have you noticed the people who are easy to talk to, joyful, infectious, and kind-hearted? They seem to attract people to them, fostering trust, admiration, and respect. This is a loving person. They attract several people for this reason. Nevertheless, this is only one example of a loving person. Scores of people will have their own unique, loving traits that attract others. Now, let's compare my example person to someone who lacks love. This person is boastful, argumentative, condescending towards others, judgmental, and dismissive of those with whom they disagree. How many people will they attract compared to the loving person? In my opinion, very few. This illustrates the strength of love over being unloving. Even in less extreme cases, the result will be consistent.

I feel we find ourselves at a critical juncture in history. It's becoming progressively apparent that positivity and love are increasing within us. However, negativity appears to be intensifying but within fewer people. Love will flourish, and more people will embrace it in the future. The outcome is unavoidable. Love, if it hasn't, will soon emerge as the dominant force for humanity.

It is crucial for every individual to continuously broaden their behaviours of love and thereby attract greater levels of loving energy.

Chapter 14: A Level Up

Love, when combined with consciousness, moulds our reality. This transformation occurs at an individual level and simultaneously influences humanity. As we expand our energy of love through our unique thoughts, beliefs, goals, and dreams, this amplified energy encompasses not only our physical form but also our mental being. This growth leads to healthier bodies and a broader consciousness. Our love energy expansion transcends our physical existence as it attracts universal energy being sent to us of like kind and strength. As our love deepens and becomes central to our being, the energetic aura of the heart that envelops us expands and strengthens. This field of energy intersects with the energy fields of others, the universe, and those energies interact.

Sometimes, when we walk into a room, a particular individual immediately draws our attention. Often, this effect is mutual. Our heart energy fields cause this interaction. Once our love energy expands, our field will interact on differing levels with many people in a room. This is the power of love. Love never threatens; it always conveys care, kindness, and trust. It would not be love if it did otherwise, and our hearts recognise this.

This is why we should attune ourselves to what our heart's energy field is telling us. Trust that initial message. Acknowledge and embrace these initial messages before our emotions and other thoughts overshadow them. Allow your heart and mind to work together, with your heart taking the lead. Allow your heart to signal whether it is a message of love or one that is unloving. Your heart will always recognise the difference. Have you noticed how certain individuals don't sit well with you? People have said they found them creepy, untrustworthy, or they disliked them. This can be your heart energy field and intuition informing you about that person. Nevertheless, you need to be aware and not jump to conclusions.

Your mind is a repository for all that you have experienced. This is important for recognising dangers you have experienced, like me as a child putting my finger in a candle's flame. But your mind can mislead you and often does. You may have had a terrible experience in a swimming pool as a child. As a result, your mind may tell you that every swimming pool is dangerous and you should avoid them. Your brain does this by creating specific chemicals in your body that create your emotional reaction. Logically and realistically, we know this is not true. Likewise, it is important to ensure our thoughts regarding a person we just met not be coloured by experiences or memories. Make sure that your mind doesn't quickly override the heart's message by making you react emotionally. We often allow our minds to override such heart messages automatically. Go back and focus on the initial message. Dive into them to discover their source, then analyse your thoughts to gain a deeper understanding of those messages. We should trust our hearts and consciously push our minds to use critical thinking and to understand our heart's message.

When we expand our love through our thoughts, words, and actions, where our actions encompass loving behaviours, self-love, self-esteem, and our heart, we will truly move into a higher level of consciousness.

By definition, ascension can mean the process of rising to a position of higher success. Although I am not fond of using the word, as it carries numerous connotations and preconceived images, people often use it in connection with humanity's upcoming shift to a higher consciousness.

Chapter 15: Our Higher Consciousness

Many people say that our next higher level of consciousness is that we as individuals will expand into a 5th dimension. I will not mix in the 5th dimension with a physicist's explanation of the 5th dimension. My discussion will centre upon the evolution of humanity to our next level of conscious awareness.

People observe we live in a four-dimensional world of space and time. Time is the tool for measuring our accomplishments in this reality. We often see time as being linear. Examples: I need to start driving at 5:30 PM to pick up the takeout food at 6:00 PM, or my tenth birthday was twenty years ago today and was held in this same room. As stated simplistically, we perform a myriad of things during our lifetime in a three-dimensional material world along with a perceived fourth-dimensional linear timeline - hence the space/time concept.

As our individual and collective love energy grows, we will move into a state of heart-centred living. Once we reach a threshold of love energy that generates a high vibrational frequency within us, our view of life and the universe will transform. Just to clarify, the 5th dimension is not a different place from where we are. It is an expansion of who we are in the here and now. The 5th dimension is a higher energy field that provides infinite possibilities in our reality. When your vibrational frequency matches the 5th dimension, you gain access to its properties. This is a synergy of energies. It will allow you access to the energy of the quantum field. An interesting quality of the quantum field is that it responds and reacts to your thoughts and words. Once you are expanded, you will obtain the ability to create your reality with your thoughts. Likewise, your thought processes will expand to encompass the new realities of the 5th dimension. Each of us embarks on a unique journey, contributing to humanity's evolution.

There are multiple descriptions written and online that describe what these changes could be. Studies have documented these changes in specific areas. The following is my list, in no particular order, showing some of what I believe we, as individuals, could expect as we expand our love energy and encompass the 5th dimension.

1. Expanding our heart and love energy, and combining it with our healing of self-love, self-esteem, and our behaviours, will increase our awareness and sensitivity. This awareness and sensitivity will apply to ourselves and others. Our heart-mind connection will grow in kindness, caring, and empathy. This will enable us to help those in need to find solutions and attain wholeness and joy.

2. We will move away from judgement, the need for external validation, and excessive materialism and use past missteps and traumas as healing lessons through self-discovery.

3. Our expanded heart enhances our focus and awareness of when another's heart and love energy are imbalanced. It provides us with insights and foresight into deceits, traumas, and unloving behaviours, increasing our intuition about the problems and the people involved. This heightened intuition will aid us in devising solutions that benefit the parties affected or involved.

4. Our connection and gratitude for nature will deepen, encompassing every aspect of the natural world, from the smallest insect to the vast oceans. This includes flowers, clouds, forests, streams, rivers, animals, and insects, etc. We will perceive our environment with a sense of wonder more than ever. Eventually, our enhanced development will extend to weather and other natural phenomena, improving our forecasting and comprehension.

5. We will expand our heart and mind connection. The brain will become integrated into a single, complete set of functioning processes. The heart will become integrated with our mind, and together, they will operate on multiple levels. As previously mentioned, each person possesses a unique energy field that intersects with the energy fields of others. As 99.999999% of the universe is energy, everything in the universe has a unique energy field. Our 5th dimension expansion will allow us to read and download these energies. With the integration of our brain and heart, we will be capable of downloading consciousness from the surrounding energy fields. We will begin to unify into oneness.

6. We will acquire the ability to alter how we perceive time.

7. Our manifestation abilities will grow in efficiency and effectiveness, enhancing not just the speed but the quality and, when necessary, the quantity.

Many of you may have noticed a sensitivity to the energy surrounding you. Whether that be:

1. Having a clear sense of individuals and being able to determine if they are trustworthy, dishonest, confused, kind or another attribute. Similarly, you might have the skill to perceive someone's psychological state and its root causes.
2. A sense of the energy permeating an area or crowd. Knowing if the energy is joyous, angry, subdued, sad, or the energy for the area is actively being depressed or energised.
3. Forecasting weather in the future at any location.
4. Perceiving someone's thoughts as they occur.
5. Spontaneity in understanding complex matters, intuitive insights, or clear visions of solutions to problems.
6. Manipulation of time perception allowing you to complete a four-hour project in two hours.

Although a short list, I believe our individual newfound abilities will vary and have nuances. If you have these listed abilities, or others, you are transitioning to the 5th dimension.

Chapter 16: The Impact on Humanity

Our individual expansion to encompass the 5th dimension is occurring now. The individuals embracing pure divine love to cause this expansion for themselves and others will increase in number and strength. While I partially explained the meaning and process on an individual level, the question remains: what impact will this have on humanity?

Less expanded individuals will perceive and sense those who are transitioning to the 5th dimension due to their energy and actions. The ones who haven't expanded will be drawn to those who did. Many won't know why they're attracted, but some will. People will begin to recognize that moving to a higher frequency means expanding through love and heart. Some people may not comprehend this attraction and feel compelled to be near someone radiating an aura of love. Others will watch and listen to individuals who embraced the 5th dimension and seek their insights.

By being themselves, individuals in the 5th dimension will cultivate and advance humanity through their presence, behaviour, and interactions. Given my thoughts on humanity's current phase, I think this evolution will happen quickly.

The Power of Love[2]

The self-imposed limitations, negativity, judgments, lack of self-love, and low self-esteem are dampening the love that resides within each and all of us. Lower frequency energies are no longer hindering people as much as they did decades ago. Previously, we advanced one person at a time. However, now is the time we will collectively be liberating ourselves as we expand into the 5th dimension.

Despite our unique talents and desires to expand, three things apply to each of us:

1. You must look forward with positive thoughts, set your various life goals and feelings, and know how joyous each will be. Visualise achieving each goal and experience the true impact it would have on you. Let that moment live within your mind and heart.

2. It's essential not to linger on the negative aspects of the past or present. No matter how hurtful or regrettable, it's time to stop letting these events control your life. Those events were terrible, but they are in the past. It's time to build a brighter future. You must recognize that if you don't take action, no one else will. Seeking professional help may be necessary, yet the effort and change must come from within you.

3. You must recognise those external forces that create fear and worry. These will be sources of negativity, promoting stories of doom, anger and hate, self righteous judgements, and harmful actions against others. These things lack love and heart. It is important you distance yourself from any negative energy influences, whether they come from family, friends, colleagues,

acquaintances, media, religious institutions, or political figures. Such sources of low-frequency energy will hinder your capacity for love and your heart.

Every step you take will build upon the last step taken, and your path will become easier. Every time you raise your frequency, you raise yourself. I know this may appear daunting to achieve. I encourage you to consider any part of my recommendations within this book, viewing each as a progressive step. None present insurmountable challenges. In the same vein, reflect on my recommendations and realise the extent of your progress. Always remember to recognize and express gratitude for your accomplishments.

Similarly, every step you take generates a ripple of higher energy that extends beyond your immediate perception, exerting a stronger influence on those nearest to you. As your heart and love expand, so too does your higher frequency, affecting humanity at large. Consider the analogy of a pebble dropped from two thousand feet above the mid-Atlantic; its impact creates ripples that affect only a small area. Now, imagine a mass as large as a mountain dropped at the same point. The resulting tsunami would affect coastlines hundreds of miles distant. Your energy ripples and amplifies, raising the frequency of those people close to you. The greater your love energy grows, the more people you will affect. Just by being you, your energy will influence humanity. First, your family, then your city, country, and the world. Now, imagine what a million people like you would achieve.

Chapter 17: In Our Name

We are accustomed to obeying various authorities. Controlling a population that accepts authority is easier, as those who accept authority tend to agree with those in power. Specific authoritarian institutions, both past and present, have indoctrinated many into a state of unquestioning compliance. We seldom question "follow our rules" and follow what we are told under the assumption that it makes our lives easier. Have you observed the state of our world? The two major authorities in our lives, religions, and governments, had thousands of years to perfect their systems, yet they continue to fall short.

Experience shows us that leaders are fallible and make mistakes, just like anyone else. Yet, why do we readily accept religions, governments, corporations, and political parties as the ultimate arbiters of many truths? If you follow without question, this implies that you are saying the myriad of other global leaders and religious leaders must be mistaken if they disagree. Yet, governments, corporations, and even less so, do religions and political parties agree with one another. Amidst such disagreements, how can any rational individual trust their leaders are correct most of the time? People often defend "our side" without knowing if leaders are right or wrong. Problems arise when our corporations, political parties, government, or religion are wrong and are not on our side. The actions of our corporations, political parties, government, and religions can impact us negatively, and their actions reflect directly on us. We need to create greater awareness and accountability for what our corporations, political parties, governments, and religions do.

What I observe is that many individuals are unable to provide solid or logical answers for their government's, political parties, corporations or religion's actions. People just repeat the propaganda statements they have been given or claim ignorance. If these answers reflect what you know about your government's, corporation's, political party's, or religion's statements, actions, or beliefs, then our world being in a mess is also your fault. I understand some of you won't like this statement. Nonetheless, what other answer is there? It's the government's fault? Without knowledge of an authority's actions and reasons, supporting them means you have no right to only blame them or others. By giving someone the authority to act on your behalf, others see you as being "one with them".

Numerous attacks on citizens worldwide occur for this reason. The assailants do not target our political parties, governments, corporations, or religious leaders; instead, they target us. This happens because the people gave their religions, governments, corporations, and political parties the power to act on their behalf.

Often, because of propaganda, we blame anyone who attacks us, labelling them as "stupid" or "evil". We seek revenge, believing we did nothing to provoke the attack, and question why they targeted us. Our reactions are often excessive. If we identify their race or religion, people frequently create prejudices against the individuals of that race or religion, regardless of their country of residence, how long they've lived there, or the millions worldwide. This indiscriminate dislike is illogical from my perspective. However, multiple examples of such behaviour exist.

We do this; others do this. Yet, when individuals engage in such behaviour, they add to the puzzle of why their citizens are disliked. We are not victims. Whether or not we accept the idea, we are willing participants. We support what our governments, political parties, corporations, and religions do on our behalf. If they act badly, we suffer the consequences, not them. Shouldn't we understand what is being done in our name?

Similarly, our citizens as government, corporate and religious employees have carried out many negative actions in our name here at home and overseas. We need to understand why others hate us, regardless of where we live. Finding and acknowledging what we allow to transpire through our ignorance and unkindness is important. We can correct the situation by bringing love, understanding, and freedom back into the lives of the people we harmed. If this costs us effort and money, so be it. I believe a loving individual or group would admit their harm and offer restitution. We expect no less from our laws when this occurs in our own backyard.

The Power of Love[2]

In the end, we are One.

Chapter 18: Other Dimensions

Physicists who postulate string theory state that spacetime would need to comprise ten dimensions. However, another speculative form of string theory, known as M-theory, requires the existence of eleven dimensions. These additional dimensions arise as an intriguing outcome of the mathematical coherence that string theory requires.

Scientists propose eleven dimensions, while spiritual explorers often suggest thirteen. All groups have their own reasons for their beliefs. The general agreement is that there exist more than five dimensions.

As we progress as individuals, advancing into higher dimensions, possibly the tenth dimension or higher, I am of the belief that both our physical and conscious selves will experience continued expansion. Eventually, morphing into who knows what. Beings of pure energy? Maybe, but nobody knows for sure. Despite uncertainties, we are embarking on a grand journey together.

I believe that as our love and light continue to strengthen, we experience a pulling force that will bring us into the 5th dimension.

The Power of Love^2

I will give an analogy to help visualise what is happening. All energy has a frequency. As we expand into the 5th dimension from the third dimension, our frequency moves higher. Likewise, if we go back to the third dimension from the 5th dimension, our frequency lowers. Frequencies gradually increase from low to high. Picture this gradual increase as being like moving up your dimmer switch on a light bulb. Then, picture yourself as a point of light, which increases and decreases in brightness when you move higher or lower in a dimension or between dimensions respectively.

I stated we expand into the 5th dimension. Here is how I picture this shift. We are a light that is firmly within the third dimension. As beings of light, our brightness reaches the fourth dimension, intertwining us with time. As we amplify our love energy, we increase our brightness and raise our vibrational frequency. As the 5th dimension has a higher vibrational frequency adjacent to our current space/ time state, our like energies attract. Our frequencies become synchronised with the 5th dimension, thus facilitating our expansion into the 5th dimension.

Once we reach the centre of the 5th dimension, as our light did within the third dimension, our light will then shine into the next dimension, the sixth and higher. As the fourth dimension is time, and we are already in it, our expansion to the 5th dimension will, by its very action, have us encompass the entire fourth dimension. While we are expanding into the 5th dimension, we still remain within the first, second, third and fourth dimensions. These dimensions are required for us to still be functional in the 5th dimension.

The Power of Love[2]

As we begin to expand into higher dimensions, we will stay physically present within the lower dimensions. In the 5th dimension, we are physical and energy beings, with our energy component expanded. We still rely heavily on space and time functionality.

Nevertheless, expanding into the 5th dimension doesn't mean needing all lower frequency dimensional functionalities. As previously mentioned, our abilities will undergo conscious and energetic transformations. For instance, this will cause a change in our personal interactions. As sentient beings, I believe we will become more of an open book to those around us. Harmful intentions, past traumas, and our hierarchical separations will become increasingly transparent and become a focus for us to heal. Many will deeply understand others in the third dimension without guesswork or doubts.

Our hearts and love are the gateway to expanding into the 5th dimension. There is a reason for this. It is the path forward to rid ourselves of many of the root causes of suffering for individuals and humanity. Humanity keeps professing the importance of peace and freedom. Once in the 5th dimension, our love, empathy, and caring can remove much of the suffering we face. We will be loving beings of understanding, unity, and healing. Further, with the quantum field responding to our thoughts, we will have the ability to create more quickly and thoroughly. This is why our expansion into the 5th dimension will become the next major step for humanity. I use the word, next, as I do not doubt there will be other lessons to learn as we move forward.

Chapter 19: Fearing "The Dark Gets Darker"

As we transition into the 5th dimension (I will use the 5th from now on), some people may resist embracing their hearts and love. One can identify them through their anger, hate, and desire to physically harm those they oppose. It does not matter the cause of such hate because it means they have moved away from love. I recommend distancing yourself from such people. However, it's important to know that this won't always work.

As more people move into the 5th, certain groups will become much angrier. They will become much darker than they were. It will appear as though some have lost any grasp on their sanity. This results from them creating a "like attracts like" energy feedback loop with the universe. Nonetheless, there is that ubiquitous silver lining that keeps showing itself. As an increasing number of individuals expand into the 5th, it will encourage others to shift. It will be hard to counter the loving energy fields of those in the 5th. Though individuals may darken in their beliefs, they are not devoid of light. They, too, love specific people and remember joyous times throughout their lives. Our ability to help will be especially true for those close to us, such as family members, friends, neighbours, and co-workers. It's harder to resist the change if you're not aligning with the majority. This holds particularly true when facing people close to you who show you love, kindness, empathy, and compassion. They will bring out those joyous memories and your love for them.

Humanity's rapid expansion into the 5th will significantly diminish those who dwell in such shadows. This pattern is evident when societal beliefs and opinions change. Historical instances such as women's suffrage, the end of school segregation, acceptance of interracial marriages, and gay rights faced widespread opposition, but they have since become broadly accepted. Similar events will happen with us expanding to the 5th but at an accelerated rate.

I was reluctant to focus on "the dark gets darker". However, I can see the dark is intensifying, instilling fear in many people. Nonetheless, it's not as dire as it appears. The news media has concentrated on such events, amplifying a false image of frequency and severity. I suggest shifting your attention away from the news and towards enjoyable activities. Further improve your daily outlook by writing four things you're thankful for each evening. This practice can effectively dispel many of your lingering fears from news events.

If you're reading this, you're likely on the path to expanding into the 5th, as this book doesn't attract those who lack love. Embracing love and your heart, and ascending to the 5th, is an effective way to sidestep the fears and worries propagated by unloving individuals or other negative sources, such as the news media. Revisit the chapter "Our Higher Consciousness" to remind

The Power of Love^2

yourself of the benefits you will gain in the 5th. Your heart and higher consciousness will alert you to any dangers well before they arise, allowing you to steer clear of them.

Chapter 20: Individuals Who Stay in The Dark

People ask me, "What will happen to the people who are left behind?" By "the people", they mean the individuals that do not expand into the 5th. It is an interesting question, but it contains a falsehood that is misleading. Remember, we don't move anywhere; our love and consciousness are being expanded. Yes, our frequencies move higher, but this is our vibrational rate, not a physical teleportation. The answer is that everyone will still be here and interact. However, our perceptions of reality will differ.

An individual who has evolved into the 5th will mostly be heart-centred beings with an expanded consciousness. They are loving, kind, compassionate, empathetic, and caring. Nonetheless, they will not be naïve. Many people will do everything in their power to help those who have not yet evolved to shed their anger, hate, prejudices, feelings of superiority, or intentions to harm others. Their presence alone will release tension.

Humanity will require time to adapt to and perfect their new or current abilities. As with any skill or talent, practice is necessary, especially to discard obsolete paradigms that are no longer useful and hinder progress. Some people may find this transition challenging. Nonetheless, embracing this change with love and compassion will ground us and provide the clarity needed. Remember, your struggles do not have to be faced alone, unity will bring together people to find your solutions and to support you. No one has to be alone.

To prepare for your expansion into the 5th, I recommend you contemplate the changes and become aware of the individual and societal implications. There will be numerous implications. On a personal level, these challenges should not be difficult to overcome if we work together. However, resolving issues on a broader human scale will require more time, even with a collective human effort.

I am unable to identify or suggest various solutions because I lack the answers for many of humanity's harmful behaviours. However, I believe that if enough qualified individuals collaborate and put their minds together, they will discover the solutions. It's always intrigued me that most people give up finding solutions to our issues because they can't conceive of any, leading to apathy. I often encounter remarks like, "What do you expect me to do?" or "We can't change anything, so why bother?" or "It doesn't affect me, so why should I care?" In my view, such attitudes show a deficiency in love, unity, and critical thinking. Even if we as individuals do not know the answers, I believe we should at least recognise the problem and actively demand solutions.

The affluent nations have the capability and resources to address many global issues. If they worked together, humanity could make substantial headway. However, they often require a firm push to act. The responsibility falls on us as citizens to demand these changes in democratic countries. What actions can we take? We can prioritise humanity's challenges when casting our votes. Instead of supporting candidates indifferent to these problems, we should vote for those who are committed to addressing them. If there are none, find someone.

While I understand this view may seem simplistic, I recognise responses like "What do you expect me to do?" or "We can't do anything, so why bother?" are unloving, self-serving and lazy answers. I'm confident others can solve the issues, even if I can not.

Chapter 21: Crime and Justice

Crime, criminal behaviours, and what justice entails have been hot topics for decades in many countries. Now is the time to closely examine these items.

What causes most crime? Here is my shortlist:

1. Poverty means a lack of food, shelter, clothing, or transportation for themselves or their family and friends.
2. Low self-esteem can lead individuals or groups to desire what others possess, driven by a belief that they are entitled to it. This stems from deficiency, power, envy, or a wish to feel superior.
3. Addictions often drive individuals to an overwhelming need to get what they are addicted to, leading to theft, burglary, or harmful behaviours.
4. Vengeance or revenge means getting retribution against another person for the harm caused to the one seeking revenge.
5. Superiority means the need to put others down or subjugate them through slavery, poor working conditions, forced sex, intimidation, confinement, or sanctions.

The Power of Love[2]

We are aware of the poor treatment of individuals in various cultures. This has been occurring for millennia. A prime example is the wealthy and powerful abusing people to increase their wealth or power. This applies to individuals, families, corporations, religions, cultures, and countries. Our history and current times are replete with examples. Countries often attack other countries to obtain land, resources or to force their cultural norms. Religions go on so-called "holy wars" to subjugate people of differing beliefs. Corporations underpay their employees, force long hours of work, or ignore health hazards. Individuals attack others because of differing ideological beliefs, including political, gender, sexual orientation, race, religion, education, or culture.

Regrettably, the crimes and the responsible parties go far beyond what I listed. So, what is the solution? Need I ask? The answer is Love.

Everyone behaves in accordance with (a) what they have been taught, (b) what power they believe they hold, (c) what is important to them, or (d) what they fear. Despite its simplicity, I wanted to highlight these points.

Fear, although last on the list, is frequently the underlying cause of the other listed items. Fear is employed to enforce what we are taught, such as our customs, religious beliefs, political ideologies, or social status. Deviating from the norms of one's family or community often results in discrimination, anger, ostracism, or even death. Similarly, those in power are motivated by fear - fear of losing power, threat from others gaining power, or the ambition to gain more power over others. These fears are not uncommon for individuals, nations, and religious groups.

Last, most people hold certain things as important and fear losing them. Some of these items are understandable, such as food, basic clothing, or shelter. The fear of not being able to get such necessities can induce panic. It applies to those without homes, jobs, and others. Just to be clear, homelessness or being jobless can occur because of natural disasters, economic recessions, changes in technology, disease, becoming disabled, addictions, or being elderly. I could list more items, but my point is that many of these items are not within their control.

Likewise, fear comes into play when people believe they are not being treated equally and have fewer freedoms.

1. Gender is a prime example. Women fear they will not be as successful due to discriminatory wages and fewer promotions. Not that long ago, women had to fight to gain the freedom to vote, own property, or choose their education and occupational fields. The Western world experienced this, but other areas treat women worse.

2. Prejudice has always been rampant. Slavery, regardless of race or individual, has been common throughout history. Most of us are well aware of Black slavery, but conquerors have often enslaved a country's people throughout history. Even today, although we conveniently do not call it slavery, people subject millions of children to forced labour for pennies a day. Similarly, people across the globe have suffered countless harms due to religious and cultural intolerances.

3. Technological changes create fear. Losing the horse and buggy because of the automobile caused thousands of people to lose their jobs. The fear of job loss due to alternative fuel sources is causing fear in the fossil fuel industries. Similarly, automation and artificial intelligence are gradually replacing labourers, factory workers and customer service people, among others.

These widespread examples have a significant impact on humanity, and I will conclude with them. In examining these examples, our solution lies in empathy, compassion, and love. This includes removing people's fears. It is my opinion that fear drives individuals to act in harmful ways to themselves and others. Fear drives individuals to desperation and is used by others for control. Much of these mistreatments and criminal behaviours will disappear as humanity expands into the 5th.∴. Given the changes that will occur to us, we will no longer tolerate these behaviours and their causes, and we will no longer tolerate the created fears. Humanity will work together to find solutions.

People have an interesting view of justice. While I understand the emotional feelings that push people to want revenge or take revenge themselves, it will achieve nothing loving. Many people presume that locking up and neglecting individuals is the best response to their criminal actions. The problem with locking people up for a specific period is it creates problems. Authorities sentence the majority of individuals to a limited time in jail. After incarceration, individuals often emerge from jail, having lost everything. How do we expect these people to survive? It's likely they won't and may turn to theft or burglary to get what they need.

The Power of Love[2]

So, how does solely locking them up help? It often does not. If we desire to reduce crime rates, we must look for different solutions that are rooted in love, compassion, and empathy.

When individuals harm others, whether through theft or physical harm, we should restrain them but not label them as criminals. We need to recognise the majority of criminals require our help. Their acts are likely driven by fear. Whether that be for a lack of basic needs, addictions or otherwise. Society should offer rehabilitation and assistance until they amend their behaviours. Where needed, this rehabilitation should encompass training tailored to the individual's preferences and skills for prospective employment. Likewise, provides employers the opportunity to offer them jobs. Additionally, there should be strategies for providing temporary housing when necessary. The roots of these changes lie in demonstrating the significant benefits for individuals. While no one can change another person's beliefs unless they agree, their self-interest and the benefits awaiting them, including a loss of future fears, will likely change their minds. It's important to remember that some expanded individuals will possess the ability to discern the truth of such changes in people. Some of these expanded individuals could become tutors and counsellors who could facilitate changes, including assisting people into the 5th.

Many oppose these ideas, under the assumption that incarceration is the only effective deterrent and solution. How is that working? Regardless, do you believe the process suggested above would cause a person to become a criminal again once released?

Likewise, I believe we should offer rehabilitation and assistance for those in similar situations within the general population. This will often prevent them from committing a crime.

I presented parts of the solution, not to be comprehensive, but to stimulate critical thinking. Nevertheless, some countries in Northern Europe have adopted similar approaches with remarkable outcomes that are based upon empathy and understanding with the intent to heal. The reoffending rate in many Western democracies is high, but I found it difficult to get accurate numbers due to differing counting measures. Therefore, the following numbers are approximate. Nonetheless, the reoffending rate is 50% within two to three years of release from jail in the United States and 59% in the UK. Norway is one European country that has introduced changes similar to those I suggested above. The rate for Norway is 20%, which is 60% less than the United States and 66% less than the UK. Even if these numbers do not correlate to within 10%, these statistics show solutions to reduce crime exist.

Chapter 22: You Are Forgiven

Forgiveness is a state of mind and energy. Events in the past that created guilt, shame, and regret within you are often now just self tortures created by you. While guilt, shame, and regret serve a purpose, they were never meant to be a source of continuous self-torture.

There are three ways to handle guilt, shame, and regret. Only one benefits you. They are:

1. You're ignoring feelings of guilt, shame, and regret as if they are non-existent. This behaviour can lead to the conviction that no action, no matter how detrimental, requires you to feel such emotions. Those who do this lack an understanding or a desire to understand responsibility, often causing emotional distress and harm to others throughout their lives.

2. You're holding onto specific guilt, shame, and regrets from the past. Often, the harm we have assumed they've caused is minor in the grand scheme of things. Nonetheless, there are times when the person affected by your actions may not forgive you, choosing to remind you of your past, making it difficult to let go.

3. Recognising feelings of guilt, shame, and regret, understanding their origins, learning from them, and then changing who you are being. Those who do this understand that such feelings are signs of their harmful actions. You recognize the need to change your behaviours to prevent you from repeating the harm that caused these feelings. By doing this, you no longer have the need to hang onto your guilt, shame, or regrets. Nonetheless, there is an understanding that persistent efforts to change will lead to success.

Which method is for your greater good? I hope we can agree that the third method is the correct answer.

Moving forward from your past events of guilt, shame, and regret is one way to create self-forgiveness. You create this within yourself. Therefore, I will change the action from "You are Forgiven" to "I Am Forgiven", as you achieved this within you. In my opinion, forgiveness only applies to ourselves from ourselves.

We all live in glass houses and throw stones. Everyone has caused harm to another, whether unintentionally through ignorance or intentionally. Every time we harm someone, we are throwing another stone. Yet, we often pass judgment on others for their harmful actions. Many become sanctimonious, self-righteous, and pompous as if they are superior. In reality, they are still throwing stones. As stated, such behaviour is often a tool to placate their low self-esteem and boost their ego.

Likewise, they make up excuses for their behaviour. Some religions view the person's actions as a sin and condemn them.

There is a Christian bible verse I like that applies to these situations: "Judge not, and ye shall not be judged: condemn not, and ye shall not be condemned: forgive, and ye shall be forgiven." (Luke 6:37, KJV). Yet my thoughts extend to how you will help and support them. My observation would be that they are not helping the person by beating them down.

Once again, it comes back to love.

While forgiving others can be a positive first step, it begs the question: where are our hearts? I mention that forgiveness "may be a good start" because I do not believe it makes for a good ending. We often forgive someone for an action that harmed us. Observing this behaviour always pushes me to consider the following thoughts and questions regarding forgiveness:

1. We forgive people for harm, yet we still cause harm to others.
2. We often forgive, but don't forget and still judge the other person.
3. Do we feel superior for giving our forgiveness?
4. How do we show love and the desire to heal everyone involved?

We need to examine these within ourselves to determine what each of us believes forgiveness means towards another person. Once completed, ask yourself, "Is this who I desire to be?" Ultimately, had we not judged the person initially, we would not find ourselves in a position where forgiveness is necessary. From my perspective, forgiveness should be replaced by empathy, understanding, compassion, and caring with the intent to heal everyone involved. It is an example of where the best solution is love in action. As the song says, "Love is all there is." (Song by Sheryl Crow/ from her album Detours).

Chapter 23: Open Your Heart and Mind

I have never met someone who, after expressing their spiritual beliefs, would then instantly declare their spiritual beliefs to be incorrect. People form their spiritual beliefs over the years and shift them slowly, if at all. Individuals resonate deeply with their spiritual beliefs. For many people, their spiritual beliefs shape their identity more than anything else.

Nonetheless, we must continually adjust our spiritual beliefs as new insights emerge. In my view, spiritual beliefs cease to be relevant if they lack fluidity. Fixed viewpoints constitute doctrine or dogma rather than belief. The beliefs of humanity three thousand years ago differ vastly from our current beliefs. Likewise, our beliefs from twenty years ago should not be identical to our current beliefs. As our understanding evolves, so should our spiritual beliefs. Our world and universe are in a constant state of change. With these changes, so should our understandings change, yet many individuals resist opening their minds to adjust.

Unchanging doctrine shows a lack of open mindedness and is likely an ego enhancement exercise. Likewise, parroting others' words does not honour individual spiritual beliefs. Individuals often gravitate towards doctrines and dogmas as they find relief from the burden of independent thought. Life becomes simpler when one only needs to adhere to the teachings they have received. Nonetheless, individuals may face problems when they encounter differing beliefs that resonate with them. Mere repetition of words or book passages does not create genuine belief, but prolonged practice of this can devolve into a form of cognitive dissonance.

My concern is the lack of critical thinking and open-mindedness, which causes people to refuse to listen to new concepts or different viewpoints. This, historically, caused problems for humanity and a lack of love. Personally, I feel fortunate to have gained insights that have positively influenced my outlook on life and who I desire to be.

My observations on human behaviour may seem harsh. However, my intention is to cultivate a wider consciousness in you about how your spiritual beliefs and actions, or their absence, impact yourself and humanity. I shall endeavour to lead from a place filled with love, joy, unity, understanding, and freedom. Should I not always succeed, I ask for your understanding. I know many of you could teach me something that would shift my worldview. This is how it should be, as we each are teachers. Nonetheless, I hope to bring you distinct insights that will open you to new possibilities. I hope they help you become more of who you desire to be. Whether or not you concur with my views, I will have fulfilled my objective. Your response, whether in agreement or dissent, will solidify your self-perception. Should I inspire a single individual to improve any aspect of their life, I will consider my efforts successful as a teacher. I firmly believe that silence does not foster progress and may even make a situation worse.

By nurturing our spiritual beliefs and allowing them to empower us, we can open ourselves to the 5th and achieve spiritual expansion beyond our earlier experiences. The current trajectory of spirituality is offering us a path to peace and freedom, achieved through our hearts and our love. It is through the 5th and connecting with our oneness that we become who we desire to be.

Embrace being an adventurous and courageous spirit. Embark on a heart centred journey upon a path that is loving. Ask yourself who you desire to be, then embrace those aspirations and create you from you. Connect with your inner peace, using it as a stepping stone to reflect and embrace your love. Recognise that at your core, you are love, joy, unity, understanding, and freedom. Your conscious awareness of these core drivers will transform you.

It is my belief that we are mere shadows of what we may grow to become especially after we expand into the 5th. Then we will have the ability to entrench love, joy, unity, understanding, and freedom into everyone's lives. Nothing humanity achieves will endure if we forget these as our primary goals. We are creators, creating and changing everything around us every minute of every day. This is our innate nature. Nonetheless, once we expand into the 5th, our creative abilities will soar.

Love requires a constant conscious awareness of your being. This will allow you to transform the world through your thoughts, words, and actions. Our collective connectivity allows us to share perspectives and, in unity, use our unique selves to assist humanity. Our love, joy, unity, understanding, and freedom define the essence of humanity being One.

Please use your heart to decide if what I say resonates with you. Your heart, not your mind, first guides you to insight and understanding. Our brain is a great repository that correlates and reiterates what we have learned. Yet, it is not always helpful in deciding who we want to be, as our hearts are the doorway to love.

Challenging our spiritual beliefs requires courage, and it takes bravery to overcome our deep-seated fears, illusions, and the walls we build around ourselves. Open-mindedness makes it possible. Be open to listening to others. Be flexible and willing to modify your spiritual beliefs when new insights resonate with you. Release what you hear if it doesn't resonate with you. Use your heart and love to foster determination and embrace your truth. Settle for nothing less. I urge each of you to become a courageous spirit by keeping an open mind, respecting all spiritual beliefs, and resisting those who wield fear to control you. You have nothing to be afraid of. Become love and understanding and seek unity with one another. It will set you free.

Chapter 24: Oneness

Oneness is a term used most often in spiritual circles regarding humanity and means the fact, quality, or state of being unified, whole, or "One". Oneness will become our reality as we expand into the 5th. The concept of oneness will foster individual desires to address humanity's widespread challenges. This will occur at both the individual and general population levels. Unity among humanity will inspire us to work together as One in love and minimise harm to everyone. Although resolving these issues will be costly, they are the costs that love and our hearts will deem necessary. We will now consider global issues as our own.

Over the past two decades, it has become clear that our actions and inactions have a direct impact on our quality of life on this planet. Once, people assumed polluting oceans and the atmosphere had no consequences. Today, the vast majority acknowledges that climate change is real and is an ongoing significant threat.

Sadly, pursuing money and immediate personal gain often takes precedence. Humanity is relentless in its goal of making money, often overlooking the consequences of its actions.

Humanity tends to ignore issues until we are on the brink of disaster. Despite imminent climate change problems, people still choose to look away. As money and greed seem to be a driver for minimal action, it is evident that many corporations and governments do not have the general population's interest at heart. It is a possibility that hundreds of millions could be displaced from their homes and livelihoods. The likelihood of this scenario is becoming more evident with the rise in severe storms and droughts. Likewise, I believe as land ice continues to melt, coastlines are at risk of being submerged under many feet of water by rising sea levels.

Some individuals contend the cost of reducing carbon dioxide emissions to combat climate change would exceed our financial capabilities. If so, why the reluctance to invest any funds at all? The likely reason is reluctance to part with any money for personal wealth.

Ultimately, it boils down to greed and selfishness. This extends beyond corporations or governments to affect millions of people worldwide. A large number of these individuals have discarded their critical thinking in favour of money or wilful ignorance. Ignorance is bliss until it isn't.

The attitude of "It doesn't affect me, so why should I care?" will come back to bite these people.

Here is just one prime example: Coastal Regions and climate change:

The Power of Love[2]

A. The increased occurrence of category 4 and 5 hurricanes and typhoons is devastating many coastal regions. Yet, people claim, "But I live inland, and it doesn't affect me." However, governments and insurers, among others, will end up paying the cost of restoring infrastructure and repairing and replacing damaged buildings. Those billions of dollars in annual costs come out of taxes and increased insurance premiums.

1. Many of these regions engage in agriculture, supplying us with food. The disappearance of these agricultural lands will drive up food prices.

2. The cost of relocating millions of people inland due to coastal flooding exceeds by billions the cost of hurricanes and typhoons.

3. I have heard coral reefs globally are crucial for sustaining many fish populations. At the rate coastal water temperatures are rising, it may not take long before ninety percent of coral reefs are dead. This would devastate oceanic fish stocks, drive up fish prices, or render some seafood unavailable. The loss of millions of jobs and the potential starvation of thousands of people is a likely result.

No country could afford the hundreds of billions of dollars needed to aid citizens after these disasters. Despite this, payments will be expected from governments as those affected cannot afford the costs. Likewise, without aid, how would neighbouring countries, provinces, or states be able to afford the added billions of dollars in aid for the relocating citizens? It would be unlikely they could achieve this.

For those who claim, "I live inland, it won't affect me", how will you remain unaffected? You will pay much more for taxes, food, and insurance to cover the billions of dollars required to manage the aftermath of disaster after disaster. Tackling climate change now is more cost-effective for us than waiting.

Sadly, there will likely be many deaths, injuries, and diseases related to these disasters. From this perspective alone, saying, "But I live inland, it doesn't affect me", shows a total lack of cognitive thinking or love.

Beyond climate change, other environmental damages require our attention. Although solving every environmental problem is challenging, we must focus on the most serious issues, like climate change, that directly and immediately affect life on our planet. Yet, we should not disregard other matters.

The long-term accumulation of heavy metals, such as mercury, lead, arsenic, and cadmium, can cause serious illnesses and even death. Have you heard of 2-butoxyethanol, ethoxylated nonyl phenol, methylene chloride, naphthalene, toluene, trisodium nitrilotriacetate, or xylene? They are chemicals found in some household products which are known to be harmful. It is unfortunate, but the list of harmful substances is endless. Toxins are either carelessly discarded into the environment or intentionally incorporated into our household products. It comes as a shock to health-conscious individuals when they fall ill because of an accumulation of these toxins in their bodies.

Over recent decades, the incidence of cancer has continued to escalate despite a large decline in smokers. Our responsibility for the escalating death toll from environmental poisons should weigh on our conscience. Our capacity to damage life on earth does not stop with chemical poisoning.

In previous chapters, I've provided a long list of unloving abusive behaviours that impact humanity. I won't repeat them again here. Nonetheless, other harmful actions by humanity include overfishing, deforestation of rainforests, degradation of rivers and lakes to facilitate urban expansion in arid areas, and converting wetlands into urban territories, to mention just a few.

Can you now understand why our actions create concerns for millions of people? Sadly, few of us have shown interest in thinking about or exploring these matters. Now that we are expanding into the 5th, love will push us toward unity and oneness. The concerns outlined in this chapter indicate that many people are indifferent to the well-being of the rest of humanity. Equally clear is that this outlook is shortsighted and, as the adage goes, "You are shooting yourself in the foot." (Originator Unknown, attributed in WWI).

As we move into the 5th, we will not ignore these harmful and unloving situations because our hearts and minds will recognize humanity's oneness and that the harm we do to others we do to ourselves.

Chapter 25: Nationalism

I've stated this repeatedly, but the source of harm—be it an individual, corporation, religion, or government—is irrelevant. Regardless of their source, we must prevent actions that harm both society and humanity.

Nonetheless, I believe the current state of nationalism is self-serving, promoting greed and hostility among nations. Historically, this has been a recurring pattern.

Taking pride in your nation's accomplishments is a good thing, but blind allegiance is not. Many people view it as acceptable to support their country, regardless of whether the government's actions are right or wrong. I define wrong actions as causing harm to another nation. The reluctance or inability of many individuals to question or stop these actions allows governments to perpetrate harmful acts, often without facing deserved consequences.

Others dislike or even hate specific nations. I have found it takes minimal research to determine which nations are causing harm to other nations and why. While occasionally such animosity may be baseless, often there is a direct correlation between a nation's actions and the negative effects and feelings generated. Regrettably, it is common for the citizens of the nations causing harm to be unaware of the reasons behind their country's poor reputation.

Three things often contribute to this:

1. Blind obedience and loyalty to their country.
2. Ignorance due to media misinformation or lack of information.
3. Propaganda.

I will assume that items 1. and 2. are recognised and understood without explanation—however, item 3. Propaganda lacks understanding and recognition by many people.

Nationalism creates a pliable mindset within a population, increasing people's susceptibility to manipulation via propaganda. It's a common misconception that propaganda is only used by other nations. In reality, there isn't a nation that doesn't employ it. Propaganda is a strategic form of communication aimed at persuasion that affects people's emotions, attitudes, opinions, and actions for ideological or self-serving ends. Predominantly seen in politics and the media, it rarely offers objective information and often presents selective truths, if any. The deliberate use of propaganda exploits people to coerce agreement with the propagator.

Here are a few forms of propaganda you may recognize, which have been used extensively for deceitful purposes.

1. *Demonising the enemy*: Portraying countries or individuals who hold opposing views as immoral, evil, or unintelligent is a tactic

used to prejudice listeners and foster negative opinions about the vilified group. It's a psychological snare to which many fall prey. To be clear, there are instances where demonising the enemy is justified. One historical instance by the allies involved the Third Reich and Hitler during World War II, but this was not used for deceitful purposes.

2. *Deception*: Falsifying or implying the existence of documentation that supports the propagandist's stance, or by presenting and utilising selective information that solely supports their position. This propaganda has no justification.

3. *Flag-waving*: Demonstrating justification on the premise that supporting them by waving your flag, playing an anthem, or pumping up your country's achievements (or similar) is proof of your patriotism and a sign you support your country. Such activities do not necessarily demonstrate patriotism, as it could be an act to deceive.

4. *Labelling*: Labelling individuals or groups with terms like unbeliever, evil, racist, socialist, or communist can be used to discredit them, casting them as undesirable. This tactic is often used by supporters of opposing political parties or nations without any factual basis.

5. *Out of context*: The practice of using selective quotes to portray opponents as uninformed or weak involves taking statements out of context. For example, the quote "I am not for abortion" was given without context. The complete statement specifies it does not apply when an abortion is needed to save the mother's life. This propaganda has no justification.

The Power of Love[2]

Every day, our Western World bombards us with propaganda. It's crucial to recognize and sidestep it, as it presents a biased perspective that doesn't foster unity, understanding, or freedom. Western democracies pride themselves on their freedom, and we hold freedom as a vital aspect of our lives. Yet, one must question the extent of our freedom when our government, political parties, and media use deception to win our agreement.

While I support freedom of speech, I don't believe that a caring and loving individual could justify propaganda. Just because you can do something doesn't mean it's right. We should point out the people who use propaganda for their misleading and harmful actions. This is especially true if our goal is for oneness, understanding, and freedom for everyone.

What has happened with our critical thinking, and when did we give up on caring for our ideals? Are democratic governments formed to push their nations or party's agenda regardless of who it harms? Governments and political parties often no longer serve the people. Many reinforce and empower groups that only support them. Often, hardcore supporters are driven by a continual stream of propaganda. We can spot how well the propaganda works by the number of supporters who quote it.

When we slander and vilify others or entire nations for our gain, it contributes to international strife. Similarly, using your nation's power, whether it be financial and/or military, to force deals with other nations is being a bully. Such actions do not differ from how a schoolyard bully behaves. Bullies who, because of their size, strength, and threats, often ridicule, physically abuse and/or steal from other students. There is no difference except in size and scope. Yet, we become hypocrites when we accept these actions of our country but do not accept them in a schoolyard.

Much of our media is no better, including mainstream and alternate media sources. If the media supported freedom, they would allow us to make decisions by presenting us with all the facts rather than attempting to manipulate us with emotional and biased "opinion pieces" provided to appear factual. When news media conceals the facts and fails to provide relevant information, it suggests they are either ashamed of their opinions or lack solid reasoning to support them. Can we consider anyone who endorses such behaviour a true advocate of critical thinking, understanding, and freedom? I do not. These actions are harmful and need to be curtailed through public awareness and pressure. While the media has freedom of speech, that does not mean people have to accept or listen to what they are saying. Those spreading hate and propaganda can talk to an empty room, as we have the choice to not attend or listen. When listening, people may speak up and call the speaker out. Likewise, we have avenues to take action. For example, when the media is involved, we can contact the program's sponsors to complain and state we will not support their products. This has proven itself to work numerous times.

Suppose we, as democratic nations, wish for peace and freedom to take root worldwide. In that case, we as individuals, our political parties, media, and governments need to step up and recognise their own part in preventing us from reaching these goals. We, as loving individuals, must take the initiative to speak out with conviction. This goal is possible through education, voting, supporting suitable candidates, or engaging directly with the individuals involved.

It's vital to recognise that an ideal political party in a democracy should gain support from all regions and a diverse range of people. A lack of this broad support means they do not represent the general population. Due to people's misunderstandings, we have recently observed many democracies becoming politically fractured over these issues. This lack of support for every individual's rights and well-being shows a serious decline in our societal participation. We've retreated into unloving, self-absorbed behaviours, leading to social division and hostility.

People have been misled, and they actively oppose oneness, unity, and understanding. It's our responsibility, as supporters of oneness and unity, to seek solutions since our opponents likely won't.

Chapter 26: Re-evaluating Who We Are

Today, there's a tendency to prioritise immediate personal gain, often disregarding the importance of others unless it risks causing us undue harm. Even then, our judgment often falters. A lack of unity and understanding always leads to disaster. Understanding how our actions and behaviours affect others is vital for transforming our beliefs about who we are being.

Sometimes, we overcomplicate what oneness means. Put simply; oneness means we should not divide ourselves against one another in anything we do. Failing to consider others, exploiting situations for personal gain, and acting for our own self-interest while causing others harm is not oneness. This holds true whether such actions are taken by individuals, groups, corporations, or nations. Most people understand these behaviours foster division, resentment, anger, and hatred, which can escalate to prejudice, violence, wars, and other self-destructive behaviours. Humanity should have recognised and avoided this cycle of harm long ago. But sometimes, we are not the brightest pebbles on the beach (unknown source). Nonetheless, we can solve these collective issues by embracing the love found in empathy, compassion, caring, and unity.

I believe expanding into the 5th will have us agree on one thing: humanity must come together in peace. Expanding into the 5th involves growth and evolving in our understanding about life to form functional beliefs that benefit each of us.

Love encompasses everything that is required for peace. There is nothing about gaining peace that does not interact with love. To ignore this universal truth is detrimental to being the best we can be. The principle of unity and understanding extends beyond our physical existence to love and our beliefs. It is through our shared religious scriptures, spiritual doctrines, and current scientific insights that we can uncover the answers to achieve unity and peace. To find the solutions necessary for peace, we must step outside our self-imposed boxes and embrace the more expansive view. It is no coincidence humanity's current generations are the first to be blessed with access to vast amounts of knowledge. The gateway to genuine understanding and unity has swung open, offering us a glimpse of broader and grander horizons.

Open discussion benefits our physical, mental, and overall well-being. Your individual understanding of life and the universe comes from developing and exploring experiences that will shape your unique perspective. Openness to new information will help us evolve and become who we want to be. Employ your curiosity along with an open-minded exploration, and you will understand what re-evaluating yourself truly means.

The Power of Love[2]

The practice of critical thinking and understanding, combined with love, joy, unity, and freedom, will create a new generation of leaders. These people will lead by recognising the importance of oneness and peace.

Chapter 27: How Will We Manage in the 5th?

As we expand into the 5th, we will have the ability to create what we wish. Few people are aware of what this could mean. Society has often conditioned us to confine ourselves within false and limiting boxes, which has stripped most of us of the potential abilities we should have realised throughout our lives. We're told we're imperfect, born in sin, and face limitless impossibilities. The advice we receive is not to be "silly dreamers" and to "get our heads out of the clouds". Many individuals are yet to realise they can attain the heights of their dreams through their thoughts, words, and actions, all fueled by love.

While opening ourselves up to love is the best possible start, there is one box that encompasses other boxes and hinders our progression. We label this box as our body. People ignore their creative abilities because they are taught to identify themselves as a body. But we are beyond being merely a body with a brain. We have become fixated on the physical. We will be unable to realise even a fraction of our potential until we recognize we are energy and exude a powerful energy field that inter-reacts with the universe. And once again, we are One.

The Power of Love[2]

The idea of being solely a physical body is too limiting to account for our total functionality. Nevertheless, we continually reinforce the concept that our body is the predominant aspect of who we are. In fact, our energy field is the predominant aspect of who we are. To be clear, I am separating the body as being physical for convenience and understanding. It is important to remember that our body is 99.999999% energy.

Much of the body is used as a tool to navigate the third dimension. Nonetheless, the body contains energy centres throughout it that are required for us to have an energy field. While I have centred on the heart and brain, our energetic interactions with the universe are far more complex. Our body is imperative for survival, and we should appreciate and thank it. Nonetheless, our consciousness and our surrounding energy field being intertwined with our body's energies makes us much more than a physical body. Our energy fields make possible our inspiration, conscience, inner voice, intuition, and love. Without our energy field engaging with the world, our perception and quality of life would remain limited, much like our interaction with societal labels. Likewise, without our energy field, we could not expand into the 5th.

While important to remember that we have physical and energy field structures, recognise that they are One. Similarly, as we regarded our physical body as separate from other people's physical bodies, we know that they are also One because of our energy fields.

Humanity has always tried to break down everything into its component parts. This approach to examining everything as its component parts creates problems because the universe is interconnected, and every portion, regardless of its size, affects the rest of the universe. Quantum physics states that this total integration creates a functioning whole that is not separable into standalone parts.

Our less-than-loving behaviours developed because of what we have seen or been told. No one behaves counter to their beliefs. Our actions are driven by our beliefs and resultant fears. Metaphorically speaking, we placed ourselves in illusionary boxes, forming separations that dictate how we behave.

Our societies created thousands of separate boxes that apply to everyone, whether they are a dictator or an office worker. We allowed ourselves to be boxed in to such an extent that we don't look for a way out. Most people lack the belief there is a way out. Especially the destitute and starving millions.

Without exception, our societies placed every one of us in a set of labelled boxes, each label dictating our limits and boundaries. Humanity loves to classify everything and everyone. In every culture, our behaviour towards others is determined by their label. We assign labels to those in authority, including monarch, dictator, president, prime minister, pope, CEO, and general. The same applies to everyone else, such as the homeless, clerks, labourers, managers, priests, lawyers, doctors, artists, actors, and homemakers, etc. Then we add labels regarding a person's attributes, including their gender, race, marital status, education, wealth, religion, and age, etc.

As soon as we identify a person by their labels, we place them in a box of prejudicial assumptions. What's worse, everyone accepts these labels. Would it be that difficult to develop new concepts that promote oneness, understanding, freedom, and love without separation? If you believe it would be difficult, I ask you to throw away that thought. Love would not create separations that cause harm. Nevertheless, labels change. What happens when a person in authority retires or abdicates their power? They become just like everyone else and are individuals trying to live their life. When a person becomes severely injured or dementia sets in, regardless of their label, they do not differ from others in similar circumstances, regardless of their former societal box label. Promoting unity, understanding, freedom, and love need not be difficult, especially considering that we have effortlessly been doing the reverse using our hierarchies to control and inflict harm with ease.

If you recognize harmful behaviours in others, you have the capacity to recognize harmful behaviours in yourself. How you behave is your choice about who you want to be.

I recognise that modifying our concepts of hierarchy, authority, and control is difficult for people to conceive. Nonetheless, our expansion into the 5th will make this transition easier to understand. Remember, people will become as transparent as open books to many around them. We shall perceive their energies and observe their skills, talents, fears, and traumas. We will no longer see a title but a unique person. Likewise, our love and heart will understand and help them heal and gain energetic harmony – just

114

as others will do with us. These shifts will allow us to understand how similar we are, regardless of authority and title. Love will guide us to unify into oneness, where the titles we use will become a function of a person's role in society. Similarly, we will better understand the importance of every individual's role in humanity.

We will recognise the key roles played by the day-to-day working person, as without them we would have no buildings, vehicles, roads, retail outlets, hospitals, accounting or communication networks. It will no longer be acceptable for individuals with what they believe is a lofty title to abuse those they regard as below them. People will see and regard this behaviour as unfit for leadership.

Likewise, in the 5th, we will recognise our free will to pursue what we wish. You listen to your heart and love as you become more harmonious with life and the universe. Open your awareness, discard unhelpful beliefs, and find ones that work. No matter what your eventual choices are, joyously imagine your goals and bring them to you.

Chapter 28: The Timelines

Each person's path to the 5th is unique and will require time. It is not appropriate to judge the timing of someone's expansion into the 5th. I believe some individuals may not be consciously aware that their expansion is or has taken place.

To judge others in such matters is unkind and often driven by ego. We don't criticise a child learning to walk for not knowing how to ride a bike. There's no superiority in expanding to the 5th before others. While you should celebrate your expansion and be available to assist others, you should only assist when asked. The placement of others on their spiritual path is not for you to criticise. This is consistent with our unique spiritual beliefs, which are not subject to people's dictates.

In my opinion, expanding into the 5th is a process. As I have outlined, it will be determined through our heart and love. How much growth in our heart and love it will take to increase our vibrational frequency to achieve synergy with the 5th I do not know, but I know we must increase our vibrational frequency to do so. Nonetheless, as people expand into the 5th, we will benefit from their higher frequency.

Once you become expanded into the 5th, the additional abilities available to you are extensive. I have mentioned some that I and others believe could manifest within you. Nonetheless, it will not be a magic wand that suddenly grants your wishes. As stated, it will be a process. The skills and talents you possessed prior to your expansion are likely to determine which ones you will develop first. You will find your talents intensifying. Like any talent, new ones will need to be explored and tried before you recognise your interest or potential. Learning how to skilfully play the piano is similar. You would never have known about your talent until you tried. Likewise, if you try and it holds no interest, you will probably never explore playing the piano again.

The truly profound impact of the 5th is the higher energy field that opens up endless possibilities for our reality. As mentioned, it provides access to the quantum field's energy, which responds to our thoughts and words. This allows you to shape reality with your thoughts. Similarly, our heart-centred talents and skills will accelerate and facilitate our desire to solve many of our personal and humanity problems. These will emerge from our evolution, and just as our skills and talents require time to develop within us, so will the changes we wish to see in ourselves, our societies, and humanity.

We can compare the journey towards oneness to a light at the end of a tunnel. We can see it, but it will take time walking to reach it.

Chapter 29: Relationships and Leadership

In the chapters titled "Energy" and "Abundance", I have listed multiple behaviours. Previously, through my writings and radio programs, I have explained in detail each behaviour listed in this book. Our behaviours are central to who we are being and how others perceive us. Moreover, they serve as a feedback loop for our brain because as we decide to change and practice them, they shape us into the person we desire to become. Consistently repeating these behaviours will establish a strong neural network in our brain, making these behaviours second nature. Anyone who wishes to enhance the love within themselves should adopt the behaviours I have chosen to discuss below, which apply to both personal relationships and workplace leadership.

My selected list of loving behaviours are:

1. Authenticity:

Authenticity means being consistent in word and deed, having the same fundamental character in different roles, being comfortable with your past and what shaped you, and becoming "the person you are created to be" versus acting and/or being deceitful. Synonyms for authenticity include genuineness, truthfulness, validity, dependability, and accuracy.

The value of authenticity:

We are attracted to people who are honest and trustworthy and who speak the truth. Authenticity is what attracts us to these people. People who are deceitful, untrustworthy, and manipulative repel us. When you embrace your personal authenticity, you naturally create loving relationships and solid friendships and become a great role model for your children.

2. Competence:

Competence is the ability to do something successfully or efficiently. Being competent means that you are proficient at something or are accomplished. It also means you use critical thinking. Synonyms include ability, proficiency, accomplishment, adeptness, knowledge, expertise, skill, and aptitude.

The value of competence:

Competence is multilayered and is expressed through your ability to do what brings you joy. This will lead to being successful, proficient, and accomplished. Doing what you love will build your adeptness, knowledge, expertise, and aptitude. Yet even that is not the whole story, because expanding your competence never ends. However, once you fold in conscious awareness, critical thinking, emotional competence, feelings, and spiritual competence, you will have wisdom that comes from your feelings, your heart, and your mind.

3. Empathy:

Empathy is the ability to know, identify, share, and understand another person's feelings or thoughts. The opposite of empathy is apathy, detachment, indifference, cruelty, enmity, and disregard. Synonyms for empathy include compassion, concern, consideration, sensitivity, insight, and humaneness.

The value of empathy:

When empathetic, you see and feel from another's perspective. You will be empathetic to people whom you meet face to face or to characters you encounter in books and movies. Empathy builds your understanding and awareness. By being empathetic, you foster unity with others and progress towards oneness. As your empathy expands, you develop self-love. You build trust and respect, which increases your effectiveness, influence, and collaboration skills in all your relationships—professional and personal. You become a peacemaker because you have developed conflict skills.

Note: Empathy is highly interrelated with other behaviours, such as authenticity, honesty, respect, trust, and confidence.

4. Acceptance:

Acceptance means allowing someone to become part of a group or community and making them welcome. It is embracing someone and giving them recognition and credence. The opposite of acceptance is rejection, opposition, dismissal, and judgment. Synonyms for acceptance include welcoming, embracing, acknowledgement, recognition, and admission.

The value of acceptance:

Acceptance expresses love and occurs when you gain awareness of a fact or truth. Picture a situation where you realise someone or something is getting annoying. To judge them and act on that judgment is not being accepting. Accept them as they are, recognising their true selves from your heart. Acceptance creates a healthier, more peaceful, and harmonious you. But you must remove your lack of acceptance for items that trigger anger and judgment and increase stress. Become aware of stressful situations created by society that you may have followed blindly, but that are harmful to yourself and others.

Acceptance doesn't mean you can't speak up and respectfully disagree. Acceptance builds a unique understanding and awareness, which provides you with a deeper understanding of the patterns, purpose, and intent of situations and the people involved.

5. Respect:

Respect is a feeling of deep admiration for someone or something that is elicited by their abilities, qualities, and achievements. It also means accepting, appreciating, and recognising who a person is being. The opposite of respect is contempt, disrespect, judgment, despising, and dislike. Synonyms for respect include esteem, recognition, high opinion, admiration, regard, appreciation, reverence, and deference.

The value of respect:

We are all unique and divine, meaning that each of us deserves respect. Respect can be confusing because many people believe they must respect someone solely because of their abilities and achievements. The common belief is that respect must be earned. However, respect is essential in a loving and peaceful society and, as such, goes far beyond accomplishments.

Respect is about accepting and honouring the diversity of beliefs, thoughts, and behaviour. Key themes related to respect are the concepts of right and wrong and freedom of speech. Respect creates justice, acceptance, freedom, and understanding through the heart. The majority in any region or country often expect everyone there and elsewhere to conform to their ways. The goal is to exert control through demanding sameness. If you are different, injustices occur. People who are disrespected in this manner often receive little support to help them move forward. This lack of support bolsters a false reality that further promotes why "those" people do not deserve respect.

To demonstrate respect to all people is one of the most challenging endeavours humanity faces. Our lack of respect illustrates that we do not understand respect or its benefits. The truth is that if we don't respect others, we are confirming that we don't respect ourselves.

6. Responsibility:

Acting responsibly means making an individual commitment to causing no harm towards or regarding someone or something. The opposite of being responsible is being irresponsible, self-centred, egocentric, and narcissistic. Synonyms for responsibility include reliability, social responsibility, awareness of guardianship, and having an obligation to keeping yourself and others safe.

The Power of Love[2]

The value of responsibility:

Individual responsibility comes from the heart and is closely related to accountability. When you are acting responsibly, you understand that you are bringing love, joy, unity, understanding, and freedom into everyone's life.

Your personal responsibility extends to yourself, your family, and to all of humanity. You are your brother's keeper, which means that you come from your heart, and you seek never to cause harm to yourself or others. Responsibility ties into many other loving behaviours, including accountability, empathy, harmony, integrity, courage, and respect. Your responsibility lies in who you are being and how you engage with all life.

Responsibility is becoming aware of how your actions or inactions harm other people and ensuring that you cause no harm. Responsibility is broad and encompasses all facets of your life and awareness. It expands as you develop your awareness and behave less subconsciously. As you increase your responsibility awareness, you become a better problem solver because you are able to see and understand how everything is connected. Your insights should be free from assigning blame, guilt and shame. Your responsible insights bring understanding and, when working with others, reduce problems.

Mastering these loving behaviours entrenches love into who you are being whether in a relationship or as a leader.

The Power of Love^2

Chapter 30: Our Emotions

As mentioned before, feelings of unworthiness, low self-esteem, and a lack of self-love, can lead to negative emotions like hate, fear, and anger. Holding onto these emotions can limit your energetic potential and hinder love. We experience emotional reactions to new situations, whether positive or negative. Our emotions are a genuine, energetic response to these situations, providing us with important information. It's crucial to be aware of them and feel your way through them, but do not let them control you. It's not wrong to moderate your emotions to prevent harming others, as failing to do so shows a lack of consideration and love. However, negative emotions need an outlet, and it's advisable to release them privately with the intention of healing. If you don't release them, they often build up and become overpowering, and you can no longer contain or control them.

When others criticise us, tell us we are inferior, or harm or wrong us, issues of ego and low self-esteem emerge. We become trapped in anger, pain, and the urge to make the other person wrong. We want revenge. Although our emotional upset is natural, the desire for vengeance, while understandable, is neither healthy nor natural. It represents a deliberate choice by you.

It is important to feel, acknowledge, and release negative emotions. Ignoring strong negative emotions won't make them disappear. Problems emerge because of the emotional trauma and suffering endured over a lifetime. The unconscious mind often revisits past injustices. When faced with situations similar to previous traumas, your old emotions resurface, leading to outbursts of anger. This reaction shows your emotions are in control. Reflect on who you are in these instances. Do you wish to be perceived as someone out of control?

Our negative emotions are one aspect of ourselves requiring healing. We are taught to hide our fears and our negative emotions and that displaying negative emotions is considered uncivilised. So we hide them away, and they build up over time and explode. However, when we display negative emotions, we justify our harmful actions with an array of made-up stories. We justify our harmful actions by declaring that we deserve justice and are entitled to seek retaliation because we believe our cause is righteous. To retaliate and cause harm does not improve situations or demonstrate love. These actions satisfy your low self-esteem and ego with a display of self-serving power.

As you expand coming from your centre of love, you will learn about, understand, and heal your negative emotions. Your heart and body will repeatedly bring up the emotions you need to heal. They are informing you of unhealed emotions that need to be released and healed. You know that anger directed at others does not come from your heart. Ignoring negative and harmful emotions can have detrimental effects on both your physical and mental health, and often results in harm to others.

Deep emotional scars need to be released. Failing to do so can eventually make any of us abusive. Negative emotions are not to be feared but heeded, accepted, and examined because they signal that your emotional and mental body are not in balance. Once you heal your emotional body, you can readily accept and discharge any new emotions that arise, thereby staying in balance. By accepting and discharging past traumas, large or small, you deprive them of the power to haunt your life. By doing this, love, joy, and freedom are no longer strangers in your life.

Similarly, children are open books, and their minds are like sponges. This is why you must teach your children how to work with their immediate emotions by observing their feelings. Be aware as to how and why their emotions developed. Show them how to honour and healthily discharge their negative feelings. Teach them the benefits of coming from the heart. Remember, children are in a developmental and discovery stage. Adults often overlook many experiences that can be traumatic for children. New and possibly traumatising realisations, such as encountering death, bullying, theft, cruelty, manipulation, violence, and conditional love, can emotionally scar children. Guiding children in a healthy way through their negative emotional experiences can create a less stressful life for them.

Emotional energy must flow, or it becomes stagnant and a blockage. Once you lock away your emotional traumas, they form knots of dense energy that hinder the flow of your healthier energies, including love. Your emotional energies come out to play when you become emotionally triggered by sometimes even minor events. Like attracts like.

You must explore your negative emotions individually and discover their root causes. A quick way to achieve this is by letting yourself feel your emotions as you did originally. Keep this private to avoid disturbing others and fully express your emotions. It is only by letting them loose that you can look at, understand, and thoroughly feel them. Release and uncover the root cause of emotions by pounding a pillow and crying if necessary. Only you can uncover the events and abuse that have triggered similar feelings and emotions. You must dig them out and experience them but with the intent to accept them and heal them. However, as we expand into the 5th, this clearing will become easier, especially when working with energy workers.

Similarly, it is important to recognise what brings you joy. Loving, happy, and joyous emotions should become the predominant emotions in your life. Explore your joyous emotions individually and discover what brings you joy. This awareness will allow you to expand your joyous events throughout your life. Joy acts as a directional signpost in life, guiding you toward the path to be followed.

Let your emotions guide you, then employ your mind to understand where they're taking you and find the reasons behind it. Your emotions will light your path, enabling you to work out the details. The key is to never disregard your feelings. Interestingly, we

The Power of Love^2

use our emotions multiple times a day to make decisions. When deciding what to eat, your feelings lead you. When you listen to music, your feelings guide you. In deciding where to vacation, your feelings steer you. Embrace every feeling that your heart and body are showing you in every moment of your life, whether they be positive or negative. Pay close attention to the direction they are steering you and why. Over time, as you become proficient at reading your feelings, you find they won't lead you astray and you will find your negative emotions no longer control you.

Once you begin to understand love and your emotional signals, you will perceive an entirely new reality. Offer love and gratitude towards your emotions. Exclude nothing. This too will help you move into energetic balance and aid in bringing you peace.

Chapter 31: Vulnerability

To understand the issues I've discussed, step back and honestly observe who you are being. You cannot walk your path to create a better you if you do not know where on the path you are. You need to determine what is required to adjust what you believe is not in your highest and best interest.

There will always be individuals who refuse to change, and that is acceptable, as they are who they are. Everyone may change at some point. That is up to them, and it will happen when they decide it is in their best interest. It is not for us to judge. We have the ability to consciously decide whether to engage with them.

I may have written this book, but I am on my path as the rest of you are on yours. Do I believe I am fully in the 5th and my issues are sorted? No.

I like that answer. It helps me to discern there is more required of me. Further, it allows me to determine my desired actions and alter my path accordingly. Recognising these things and admitting them is shedding light on my vulnerabilities. People mistake vulnerabilities for weakness. In reality, they are our strength, as they show us how to grow stronger and decrease fear or anger through increased competence and confidence. If we do not recognise our vulnerabilities, how can we ever improve?

Vulnerabilities come in many forms. The actions to remove some of our vulnerabilities include expanding our love through strengthening our education, physical abilities, mental stability, emotional state, personal relation skills, and monetary acumen, among others. Remember, such changes must come from your heart and love. They should not foster obsession, neediness, superiority, or a controlling nature.

I will dive straight into discussing my current vulnerabilities. I do this because I am not afraid of my vulnerabilities. Each person has their own vulnerabilities. We are each on our own path, and each path is unique. Nevertheless, when a person is strong, they would be able to help others.

My vulnerabilities that require work on my part are:

Low self-esteem. My low self-esteem is much better than fifteen years ago, but not at my desired level yet.

Education. I have a university education and various certificates, yet I wish to gain more knowledge across diverse fields of study. Each new piece of information expands my understanding of the interconnectedness of all things.

Superiority and Ego. In my youth, and as a young adult, these two traits were overwhelmingly present. As I alienated others, I examined the reasons and realised these two aspects were to blame. Although they crop up, I now identify them and address the underlying issues each time to keep removing the cause.

Anger. Anger still flares up when I feel disrespected or see others being mistreated. Specifically, when others promote hate and superiority, these behaviours can provoke my anger. Although my anger has declined significantly since I was younger, it sometimes re-surfaces. My goal is to observe without reacting, and I will continue pursuing this.

Those are what I see as my current vulnerabilities. Nonetheless, people may point out others, and I hope they do. Likewise, I hope to be gracious enough to thank them.

I recommend taking time to identify and list your vulnerabilities and actively work on addressing them. Remember, your vulnerabilities are not flaws, but reminders of areas for self-improvement. They guide us on our path towards becoming heart-centred and loving.

Chapter 32: Working Together

Previously, I mentioned that humanity has problems I did not know how to solve. Nonetheless, I expressed my belief there are experts in the world that, if they worked together, would likely be able to find the necessary solutions. Humanity working together is a basic feature of oneness.

Studies show that having diversity and working together to solve issues are the best methods to achieve success. It is wise to surround ourselves with individuals who possess knowledge and experience in areas where we do not, as no single person can know everything.

In the workplace, we continually compare people, where one person performed well while another's performance was average. Many companies trumpet mantras such as "We expect the best from all our staff" and "Nothing less than excellence will do". Nonetheless, there are occasions where many people did not demonstrate an excellent performance, including those leaders who push such statements. Employers often say they promote these statements to push people's job performance to a higher level. From my observations, these statements decrease self-confidence, lower morale, and cause people to underperform because no one can live up to them. Similarly, with these mantras, no one will ever grade work reviews as perfect. This decreases self-confidence and morale, which then drives down productivity. I've observed workplaces that are a mix of contradictory rules and fairness.

Nonetheless, what should working together look like on the peer-to-peer level?

Working together at the individual level is essential for both leaders and non-leaders, regardless of their employer or workplace. Most of us have observed discussions escalate into heated arguments when personal attacks occur or when individuals feel betrayed, anxious, or in fear. Personal concerns, such as an ill child or a rocky relationship, can also lead to hostility or low productivity. It is important to let others know about your external stresses. Others may surprise you with their empathetic response and the solutions they offer. When we suppress our emotions due to external stress, as we have been taught to do, our internal stress will keep rising.

Honouring our anger does not mean we must lash out at others or hide our anger away. When our anger arises, it takes wisdom to pause and recognize that something has pushed our buttons. Once we take a moment to calm down, we grant ourselves the freedom to understand. Dealing with situations calmly and rationally often leads to non-confrontational success.

Letting our emotions escalate only makes the situation worse. People most often lose control and become irrational when angry and some people will deliberately try to push your buttons to make you "lose it", so they can take control of the situation. Based on my experiences, it's challenging to not react. However, there is nothing wrong with calmly and firmly expressing your anger. Likewise, be authentic and admit your mistakes where necessary with apologies.

We should respond to anger by showing love and understanding and not demeaning, hurting, or belittling the other person. Stay true to love and remain in control, no matter what you witness in others. Be honest and truthful and point out the unloving aspects of the attack. Inform the person that their behaviour is inappropriate and unprofessional. If there are bystanders, it will cause them to pause and reflect on what was said to you. Doing this brings any bystander's love and understanding into play.

Once you point out the unprofessional behaviour, bring unity and understanding to the situation as quickly as possible. Let them know you recognise their anger. People are always angry for a reason. Invite them to explain why they are angry. A good practice for defusing anger is to listen attentively, maintain eye contact, and refrain from interrupting or offering rebuttals. This will make them feel heard. Use your love, empathy, and understanding to create something productive and not destructive. Workplace fears and the resulting anger can come from a myriad of sources, including personal stress, fear of failure, humiliation, lack of respect or ability, and of losing power.

Nevertheless, the answer to anger in the workplace is to replace it with love. This would mean you help your fellow workers to succeed. Be available to help someone who has a question or is struggling with a task. Love creates a path forward for us to look after each other. Once we do, arguments will diminish. Love being demonstrated to and from all company employees will build trust and increase productivity, imagination, and dedication.

People have multiple hidden doubts and weaknesses that were created throughout a lifetime of fear and rejection. Unfortunately, they sometimes think they can offset these behaviours by attempting to make themselves appear better than their co-workers. This is why we should promote vulnerability as a positive trait and reward it. I mentioned earlier that no one knows everything, so it's smart to have knowledgeable and experienced people around us. We can only achieve this by admitting our vulnerabilities, provided there are no negative repercussions.

Humanity can cause people to be socially inept due to concepts we promote that are a hindrance to our unity. This is particularly true when we divide people into winners and losers. This habit becomes dangerous when we apply the element of winning and losing to higher-stakes circumstances that involve complex situations, such as authority, relationships, sex, wealth, power, and knowledge. While I have no issue with claiming someone as a winner or successful, I find no love in calling anyone a loser. For example, it's fine to claim a winner in sports, but what do we achieve by labeling others as losers? How does it foster working together by calling anyone a loser? In my opinion, it does not.

We must be aware of how we treat others. Success in the workplace requires responsibility for the success of others. No one is perfect in their role, and there is always something new for everyone to learn. Once we understand this, it is our responsibility to build unity by helping others. Studies show these actions drive productivity, job longevity, and trust. Nonetheless, finding fulfilment at work requires a role that challenges and allows for a sense of accomplishment. Success stories depend on the support you give to others because they return that support. This is an act of love, understanding, and oneness.

We are dealing with people, not furniture. The most successful workplaces and societies build unity, trust, and understanding at their core. When we try to force change or obedience through threats and intimidation, people become less cooperative and productive. Hence the statement: "You receive the gift you give."

Building an alternative path to a productive, loving world is within our capabilities. It is by working together through our love, unity, and understanding that we will move humanity forward to thrive. When people thrive, businesses thrive. You must work together with others to bring love, joy, understanding, unity, and freedom into everyone's lives - including your own.

Chapter 33: What Do You Want from Life?

If you are reading this book, I imagine you want to grow and expand who you are. Know that your unique insights and observations hold value. Together, humanity can work in unity despite our differing beliefs.

Some say my ideas are a pie in the sky or mere dreams, but I don't accept that. If humanity keeps setting such low aspirations, progress towards our ultimate goals will be painfully slow. Without goals, individuals stagnate. With lofty goals, we increase our efficiency and open-mindedness.

Nonetheless, to feel complete, individuals require more than just personal goals. Although personal goals are important, our social accomplishments often provide us with the greatest personal fulfilment. It's common to see individuals throw themselves into their careers, yet they may still lack a sense of accomplishment upon retirement. In contrast, those who dedicate time to raising their children, engaging in community or spiritual activities, or helping others have a higher sense of personal satisfaction. It is the balance of personal and social objectives, where both are challenging and offer personal growth, that provides a genuine sense of accomplishment.

Humanity, as a collective, is no different. The human perspective doesn't differ much from our individual perspective, but when dealing with humanity, the perspective shifts to that of a team effort. Whether engaging in an individual or team effort, we must aim high enough to drive our desires to become the best we can imagine. Our vision and desires must benefit everyone. This will allow each of us to obtain that sense of satisfaction we crave. Our desire to improve our societies can lead to this growth, which is fuelled by helping ourselves and others. Our individual desire to help others, whether focused on family, friends, community, the natural world, or humanity, will assist us in growing our heart and love.

Much of what I've written is about our need to become who we want to be. I come from an understanding that love is the engine that will drive this forward. However, I have observed that our actions rarely come from a centre of love. I hope to impress upon you that our current unloving behaviours do not drive us forward - but cause us to become like a car stuck in the mud. We can try to move it back and forth, but it often ends up not going anywhere and sinking deeper into the mud.

I do not intend to convert any of you into a likeness of me. During my life I have strived to listen and understand other points of view, which I accept when I decide they will work for me. Each person has their own path and makes choices, including myself. Nonetheless, I hold no false certainty that my beliefs and outlook are static and immoveable. I know with every step I take that parts of my understanding will change. Life revolves around growth, expansion, and change. I understand that in order for any of us to progress as loving individuals, we require diverse discussions on any and all issues. Life involves change; my understanding today differs from a decade ago. Nevertheless, let me clarify that statement. The centre of who I am has not changed. My foundation has always been and still is love, joy, unity, understanding, freedom, and faith. My approach to embodying these qualities has evolved. This is what I mean when I state how understandings evolve throughout life, and we must be prepared to alter our beliefs. We yearn for love and joy at a personal level, and in doing so, we desire them for each other.

Each of us has a unique understanding and uses differing words to articulate why love, joy, unity, understanding, and freedom are essential. Regardless of our unique journeys, the inner recognition of these values remains similar. They are our common language. Still, our present self and who we desire to become is what matters, not the path we travel. I've met atheists who embody and express these values more profoundly than some spiritual individuals I've met. Conversely, I've known many spiritual individuals who exemplify these values. I believe the time has come for humanity to undergo an evolutionary change.

I hope my words will stir your thoughts and provoke you to ask questions, and questions are good. No one person has all the answers, but that is not a concern of mine. It's crucial to recognize the problems first, ask questions, then develop solutions, and move forward in unity. Similarly, we must learn from our past mistakes to move forward.

What I've written carries a controversial tone. I think it important that we set initiatives to make positive changes in ourselves and society. My intention has been to target areas that provoke our thoughts, questions, and passions. Likewise, to raise awareness of how we can be controlled and unconscious about our behaviours. It is my belief that it's important for us to apply critical thinking and to formulate understandings to reject any false notions that we are powerless to change the world or ourselves.

There are no victims. Through our actions, inaction, and fear, we create our circumstances, both globally and individually. We cannot claim victimhood once we recognize it was our own actions or inactions that created our misfortunes. It's time to face our problems and own up to our behaviours. I often find that making these changes takes less time than expected. The process accelerates as you align with your heart, embracing love, and becoming who you desire to be. I have come to realise that many illusions and falsehoods cannot exist in an environment of love, joy, unity, understanding, and freedom. Nonetheless, recognise that your changes will not be consistent. Some may hit you like a brick and be immediate. Others will move step by step and will take longer. Similar to physical exercise, you will require rest periods to allow the changes to take full effect. This is not a race to the finish. It will take time to get to your destination, and trying to rush it forward too quickly may set you back. Be grateful for your accomplishments and expect more in the future.

The Power of Love[2]

Be mindful of what benefits you and what does not. I hope my writings help guide you towards a path of abundance through your heart and love, where abundance is joy in all facets of your life, not just wealth. Bring love, joy, unity, understanding, and freedom into your life and extend it to others. To me, this is life's grandest meaning. Personally, I am grateful to God for this insight.

Chapter 34: My Final Thoughts

I set out to write three books; they are now complete. I do not know if I shall write another book. I currently have no plans to do that.

I hope you found this book interesting. It might seem unconventional and "out there" to some people, but not to everyone. Even if you set aside my discussion on the 5th dimension, which I consider to be part of our upcoming expansion, I trust you realised the profound significance of love. Love is our next step forward for personal expansion. The core of my writings is to broaden our understanding of love and its significance for each person and humanity. In the past five years, I've written and broadcast about bringing love into your heart by observing the world, yourself, and from a broader universal perspective.

Remember, love is at your core. Understand, too, that love is the universe's most powerful force. If you have fallen in love, you know how wonderful love feels. It is glorious, powerful, and overwhelming. However, that's just a small taste of love's potential. This is merely a hint of the immense, untapped love that resides within you.

The Power of Love^2

If any of my practices resonated with you, please use those practices. I outline them below as a reminder of what each practice entailed:

1. Self observation (chapter 4),
2. The foundations of love (chapter 12),
3. Removing guilt, shame, regret (chapter 22),
4. Key behaviours (chapter 29)
5. Healing your negative emotions (chapter 30),
6. List your vulnerabilities (chapter 31), and
7. Anger management (chapter 32).

I outlined some key behaviours in chapter 29. Nonetheless, the emotions and behaviours we should expand within ourselves extend beyond these key behaviours. Love also encompasses the following behaviours—honesty, trust, accountability, fearlessness, humility, integrity, confidence, grace, wisdom, divinity, and more. Every behaviour, emotion, and feeling that builds towards harmony, caring, peace, and happiness for every one is driven by love.

I provided numerous examples of what harms us and hinders our capacity to love. Yet, our own behaviours and emotions often fuel harm. Remember, harm builds disharmony, division, fear, and suffering.

Love and harm are opposites and show the duality of our third-dimensional existence. Yet, as we embrace love, it transforms our world, eradicating much of our harm. Whether or not we do expand into a 5th dimension, the outcome through expanding our love will be the same.

The Power of Love^2

Imagine a world of peace, joy, harmony, and laughter. How would it feel to experience that?

I thought it would be useful to summarise the internal and external changes we should be aware of during our expansion.

We are One. Recognise that you are not alone. Those around you are willing to help. Do not ignore other people's support, as it could be immensely beneficial. Expand your love and push humanity to be more unified. Let go of your resistance to love, as you are not alone.

Look beyond your fears and realise the reality of love in our individual and collective awareness. Media and societal structures that desire to maintain control through our separation purposefully entrench fear within us. Embracing love will dispel your fears.

Nevertheless, be aware of the coming profound advancements, both scientific and social. Social changes will involve moving beyond race, gender, cultural, and religious biases and constraints towards new methods of coexistence and oneness. From a broad perspective, I expect significant social transformations to occur in the areas of government, business, international finance, education, and various other institutions. The few individuals who influence humanity's progress mainly for their wealth and power will lose control. These institutions will undergo reform and refinement to serve us and humanity.

New scientific discoveries will vastly change humanity and unite, awaken, and inspire us. This will include advancements in medicine, engineering, energy, and climate change solutions, among others.

Your choices are powerful and can hasten our path to achieving these changes that benefit us and humanity. Each of you has the power to catalyse loving change. It requires a commitment to cause no harm, becoming consciously aware, and a willingness to assist others. Although the journey may be challenging for some, it will be easier for others. Nonetheless, this is not a race. Regardless of the personal challenges, our unity will create this new world. We are all equal, and no one is alone. Many loving individuals are eager to combine their loving energy with yours, and together, we can achieve these aspirations. By loving through our hearts and minds in oneness, we can manifest a world filled with peace, joy, harmony, and laughter. To those creating their desired selves to achieve this dream, I thank you.

And So It Is.

Thank You, and Amen.

Acknowledgements

Throughout my life's journey, I have encountered many remarkable individuals. Even those who have caused me harm were remarkable in their own right, as they taught me who I did not wish to become and increased my discernment and awareness. Each person has bestowed upon me a gift, whether large or small.

Nevertheless, I wish to express my gratitude to those in my life who have most often shown me the power of love:

This includes my mother, Doris May Campbell; my father, James Edward Campbell; and my brother, Bruce Campbell. My partners Douglas Duplissea, Stephen Russell, and Kenneth Rogerson. My friends Karen Murphy, Louise and Richard Bartz, Daniel Burns and Thomas Threndyle, Terry Sole, Deborah Coke, Benny Young, Dean Carberry, and Pauline Burns. My mentors Jarrad Hewett, Neale Donald Walsch, and Edwin Spina.

Love, Oneness...Always.

Martin Neil Campbell

About the Author

Martin Neil Campbell, a retired executive, an award-winning author, a former company owner, and a radio show host, resides in Toronto, Canada. He understands from experience that expanding our centre of love is challenging and not always embraced. Martin believes that we can advance our life paths through love and our hearts, propelling humanity to its next greatest heights. Being no stranger to hardship, grief, joy, and love, he knows these experiences have allowed him to grow and expand who he is. Martin has often said that each person he encounters has a unique story, which has allowed him to connect with the divinity of Oneness. He believes that "Every individual offers a unique perspective from which I can learn, improve my life, and gain a new worldview, to become more of who I desire to be." He believes that if we are honest with ourselves about who we are, we can achieve our fullest potential. Love is the cornerstone of his beliefs, which he regards as the highest power in the universe.

www.ingramcontent.com/pod-product-compliance
Lightning Source LLC
Chambersburg PA
CBHW031550040426
42452CB00006B/257